Common Core in the Content Areas

The Common Core is requiring literacy across the curriculum, but what does that mean for teachers of subjects like math, science, and social studies who have a lot of content to cover? In this essential book, author Jessica Bennett reassures you that you don't have to abandon all of your great content lessons and start from scratch. Instead, you can reflect on what you're already doing well and make adjustments and enhancements as necessary. Bennett starts with a clear breakdown of the Common Core ELA Social Studies/History and Science and Technical Subjects Standards for Grades 7–12 and what they actually look like. She provides a variety of practical strategies and scaffolds that you can use immediately to enhance your curriculum and meet the standards.

You will learn how to . . .

- Incorporate a wider variety of texts into your curriculum
- Teach students to use each text with purpose, whether it is for close reading, support, argumentation, or research
- Assign meaningful group work and projects without feeling that they have to take up your whole curriculum
- Help students navigate their textbooks more effectively and read for information
- Implement the four As strategy in which students absorb content, analyze information, argue reasons, and apply knowledge
- Use writing tasks to strengthen student comprehension of content
- Teach various forms of writing and the importance of text citations
- And more!

Throughout the book, you'll find tools such as unit planning sheets, daily lesson plan sheets, classroom handouts, sentence starters, and more. If you teach a content area, this must-have resource will help you meet the Common Core with ease!

Jessica Bennett is a middle school teacher in Ohio and past president of the Ohio Council of Teachers of English.

Other Eye On Education Books Available from Routledge (www.routledge.com/eyeoneducation)

Writing Behind Every Door: Common Core Writing in the Content Areas
Heather Wolpert-Gawron

Rebuilding Research Writing: Strategies for Sparking Informational Inquiry
Nanci Werner-Burke, Karin Knaus and Amy Helt DeCamp

Flipping Your English Class to Reach All Learners: Strategies and Lesson Plans
Troy Cockrum

Common Core Reading Lessons: Pairing Literary and Nonfiction Texts to Promote Deeper Understanding
Stacey O'Reilly and Angie Stooksbury

Big Skills for the Common Core: Literacy Strategies for the 6–12 Classroom
Amy Benjamin and Michael Hugelmeyer

Teaching the Common Core Speaking and Listening Standards: Strategies and Digital Tools
Kristen Swanson

The Common Core Grammar Toolkit: Using Mentor Texts to Teach the Language Standards in Grades 3–5
Sean Ruday

Authentic Learning Experiences: A Real-World Approach to Project-Based Learning
Dayna Laur

Vocabulary Strategies That Work: Do This—Not That!
Lori G. Wilfong

Common Core Literacy Lesson Plans: Ready-to-Use Resources, K–5

Common Core Literacy Lesson Plans: Ready-to-Use Resources, 6–8

Common Core Literacy Lesson Plans: Ready-to-Use Resources, 9–12
Edited by Lauren Davis

Teaching Students to Dig Deeper: The Common Core in Action
Ben Johnson

Common Core in the Content Areas

Balancing Content and Literacy

Jessica Bennett

NEW YORK AND LONDON

First published 2014
by Routledge
711 Third Avenue, New York, NY 10017

and by Routledge
2 Park Square, Milton Park, Abingdon, Oxon OX14 4RN

Routledge is an imprint of the Taylor & Francis Group, an informa business

© 2014 Taylor & Francis

The right of the Author to be identified as author of this work has been asserted by him/her in accordance with sections 77 and 78 of the Copyright, Designs and Patents Act 1988.

All rights reserved. No part of this book may be reprinted or reproduced or utilized in any form or by any electronic, mechanical, or other means, now known or hereafter invented, including photocopying and recording, or in any information storage or retrieval system, without permission in writing from the publishers.

Trademark notice: Product or corporate names may be trademarks or registered trademarks, and are used only for identification and explanation without intent to infringe.

Library of Congress Cataloging-in-Publication Data

Bennett, Jessica, author.
Common core in the content areas : balancing content and literacy / Jessica Bennett.
    pages cm
  Includes bibliographical references and index.
  1. Content area reading. 2. Education—Standards—United States.
I. Title.
  LB1050.455.B465 2014
  428.4—dc23
  2013040552

ISBN: 978-0-415-74283-2 (hbk)
ISBN: 978-0-415-74284-9 (pbk)
ISBN: 978-1-315-81389-9 (ebk)

Typeset in Bembo
by Apex CoVantage, LLC

Contents

	Acknowledgments	ix
1	**Introduction**	1
	Hating All That's New	1
	Be True to You	2
	Change as a Process—Baby Steps	2
	Examination of the Main Course	4
	Why Does This Even Matter?	4
	Stepping Outside Your Department, Finding a Different Content Friend	11
	References	11
2	**Relax, You're Not Starting Over! Here's What You're Already Doing**	12
	Introduction: I'm Already Awesome	12
	Ask Not What You Can Do for the Common Core, But What the Common Core Can Do for You	15
	Keep Doing What You're Doing	17
	Working with What You Have	19
	Preparing to Get Jiggly with It	20
	Review: What to Do, What to Do!	21
	References	22
3	**How to Make It Even Better—Yes, It's Possible**	23
	Introduction: Reflection as a Starting Point	23
	Turning Basic to Brilliant: Higher-Level Thinking	25
	Group Work Galore: Letting Students Talk	29
	Projects: Why They Keep Us Awake at Night and How to Finally Get Some Shut-Eye!	30
	Units: Why They're Important to the Common Core	38
	Review: What to Do, What to Do!	43
	References	43

Contents

4 Why Am I Teaching Middle and High School Students How to Read?   **44**
Introduction: Learning to Read or Reading to Learn?   44
Reading with Purpose   45
Before We Read, Let's . . .   47
While We Read, Let's . . .   49
After We Read, Let's . . .   52
"I Love My Textbook!" Said No Student Ever   55
Common Core: Making Differentiating Easy   57
Review: What to Do, What to Do!   59
References   60

5 Using the Text   **61**
Introduction: Because I Said So!   61
What Is a Text Anyway?   62
Primary and Secondary Sources   66
Author's Purpose and Intended Audience   67
Text for Learning: Use It or Lose It   70
Activities to Teach Students to Cite the Text   74
Review: What to Do, What to Do!   77
References   77

6 All A's! Absorb, Analyze, Argue and Apply!   **78**
Introduction: All A's, a Four-Step Process   78
Step 1: Absorb   78
Step 2: Analyze   80
Step 3: Argue   84
Step 4: Apply   86
Back to Unit Planning   89
Review: What to Do, What to Do!   95
References   95

7 Reading, Reading, Reading—But What About Writing?   **96**
Introduction: Two Peas in a Pod   96
Writing as Learning   97
Writing to Argue   99
Writing to Inform or Explain   101
Writing for Research and Writing as a Process   101
Review: What to Do, What to Do!   107
References   107

**8 Projects, Grading and Literacy?
Is This More Work for Me?**   **108**
  Introduction: Swimming in Quicksand   108
  The Release of Power   109
  Time Management   111
  Grading   113
  Planning   115
  Collaboration   120
  Review: What to Do, What to Do!   121
  References   121

9 There Is *No* Finish Line   **122**
  The Conclusion: Why You're Awesome   122
  Balancing Content and Literacy   122
  Professional Development   123
  Rolling to Crawling to Baby Steps to Walking
    to Running: Things Get Easier   124
  Review: What to Do, What to Do!   124
  References   124

  *Appendix A1: What You're Already Doing in
    History/Social Studies for Grades 6–8*   *125*
  *Appendix A2: What You're Already Doing in
    History/Social Studies for Grades 9–10*   *127*
  *Appendix A3: What You're Already Doing in
    History/Social Studies for Grades 11–12*   *129*
  *Appendix A4: What You're Already Doing in Science
    and Technical Subjects for Grades 6–8*   *131*
  *Appendix A5: What You're Already Doing in Science
    and Technical Subjects for Grades 9–10*   *133*
  *Appendix A6: What You're Already Doing in Science
    and Technical Subjects for Grades 11–12*   *135*
  Appendix A7: Verb Switching   *137*
  Appendix A8: Unit Planning Sheet   *139*
  Appendix A9: Declaration of Independence Worksheet   *141*
  Appendix A10: Graphic Organizer for Citing the Text   *143*
  *Appendix A11: Blank All A's Chart for History/Social
    Studies, Grades 6–8*   *144*
  *Appendix A12: Blank All A's Chart for History/Social
    Studies, Grades 9–10*   *146*

Appendix A13: Blank All A's Chart for History/Social Studies, Grades 11–12 ..... *148*
Appendix A14: Blank All A's Chart for Science and Technical Subjects, Grades 6–8 ..... *150*
Appendix A15: Blank All A's Chart for Science and Technical Subjects, Grades 9–10 ..... *152*
Appendix A16: Blank All A's Chart for Science and Technical Subjects, Grades 11–12 ..... *154*
Appendix A17: Graphic Connections Organizer *156*
Appendix A18: Outline for Argumentative Writing or Debate *157*

Acknowledgments

I'd like to express my endless gratitude to Lauren Davis, my editor at Routledge. When we met, I was a Boggs, and she was an Ambrose. Since then, our names have changed to Bennett and Davis, and we have had children, read and reviewed a million books and found love for our careers and inevitably became friends. Lauren, it has been an absolute pleasure working with you and all that comes from this volume I owe to you.

I am grateful to all the teachers I've worked with for their endless knowledge and friendship. I am thankful to every one of my teachers for making me who I am today. I am appreciative of Chad Dotson, who modeled not only what it means to be a good teacher but also what it means to be a good person. Special thanks go to Molly Tener and Richard Day. Not only do you keep me sane, you make me a better teacher, and for that I am eternally grateful. You are both so much better than me. Thank-you to the numerous administrators whom I've worked with, especially Bill Mullins and Bill Hunton, who as principals knew what it meant to be a teacher and how to make someone feel truly appreciated.

Thank-you to the OCTELA (Ohio Council of Teachers of English Language Arts) board of directors and members for teaching me what it means to be a professional in an ever changing profession. Thank you, Cindy Bowman, who began encouraging me to write a book so many years ago. I'm so sorry we didn't have the chance to do it together as you wanted. This is for you, more than for anyone. I am grateful to Michele Winship, the woman I want to be when I grow up.

Finally, thank-you to my parents for instilling the belief in me that education is the only option. To my dear husband, Jason, thank you for your endless support. Every time I wanted to give up, or thought I couldn't do it, you would give me the gentle push I needed . . . or the coffee.

Meet the Author

Jessica Bennett is an 8th-grade language arts teacher at Brookpark Middle School in Grove City, Ohio. She is a past president of the Ohio Council of Teachers of English Language Arts (OCTELA); she previously served as president, vice president, and membership chair. She presents at local and national conferences and is the recipient of numerous awards, including the Leadership Development Award from the National Council of Teachers of English (NCTE), as well as Teacher of the Year from Norton Middle School, South-Western City Schools and the School Bell Award. She received her masters of education in literacy from Ashland University in Columbus, Ohio, and her bachelor of arts in English literature from Capital University in Columbus, Ohio. Jessica also has TESOL Endorsement from Ohio State University and has undergone SIOP® Training.

CHAPTER

Introduction

Hating All That's New

I admit it, I hate trying something new. I've had the same favorite restaurant for 15 years, I've never had anything but one salad, one dish and one dessert. Why mess with a good thing? I travel to the same vacation spots and shop at the same stores to ensure that I can quickly find frozen edamame or butterscotch syrup. I can only imagine the damage that would come to humankind if I were to venture down the wrong aisle and spend hours futilely searching for whole grain spaghetti noodles or return my cart to the wrong location.

I'm a creature of habit. Routines work for me. That being said, I realize that to be a successful teacher in the 21st century, I must wander into a world unknown or perhaps, in my case, tiptoe. This book is intended to help you tiptoe—or, if you prefer, stomp, jump or skip—into a world that may be slightly new, unknown or at the very least, constantly changing. If you're like me and hesitant to try something new, the following chapters will show you how to take the wonderful lessons, strategies and activities you're already using and adapt them to meet the reading and writing demands of the English Language Arts Common Core Standards for History/Social Studies or Science and Technical Subjects, Grades 6–12.

If you're the type of person (unlike me) who is exhilarated by trying new things, this book is for you too! This book will give you a wide variety of new tools to use in your classroom to help your students become prepared for college and the ever changing workforce of the 21st century. The Common Core Standards don't just help prepare students for what lies ahead; they give teachers the opportunity we've been waiting for to help students explore their interests and prove knowledge by doing more than filling in bubbles.

Be True to You

This book is not intended to make you an English teacher. It is intended to give you the skills you need to ensure that your students are prepared to meet the demands of the Common Core Standards. However, no matter your subject area, you will inevitably be a teacher of English. Another goal of this book is to ensure that reading and writing do not take away from content knowledge but rather apply and prolong it for every student in your classroom.

Although the lessons and activities in this text are directly linked to the Common Core Standards for History/Social Studies and Science and Technical Subjects, Grades 6–12, most of the strategies can be easily adapted to the reading and writing demands in any content area, including Art, Wellness or Physical Education. The activities and strategies provided in this book will focus on engaging students in the learning process that is directly related to reading and writing. Robb (2003) states that "engagement with a text—whether the text is written, oral, or visual—involves that same active, constructive exchange between the known and the new" (p. 23). This text will provide teachers and students with adaptive strategies for the known and introduce new tools that can be used to meet the demands of 21st-century learners, regardless of the content area.

Change as a Process—Baby Steps

This book begins by giving you an understanding of the basic components of the English Language Arts Common Core Standards for History/Social Studies and Science and Technical Subjects, Grades 6–12. Let's face it: the first step in trying something new is getting to know it and being prepared for the change. That's exactly what the beginning chapters will help you master. This book will go on to give you examples of how you are already implementing many Common Core Standards in your classrooms. It will hopefully make your lessons more purposeful and, if needed, help you prove to administrators and others that you are preparing students for 21st-century college and career demands. Your lessons will demonstrate higher-level, collaborative, problem-solving students. Each chapter will begin with a short introduction and end with a quick review of what was covered.

The ensuing chapters will go on to help you take what you're already doing and make it better. I know—it seems unbelievable, right? They will lead you to an understanding that teaching reading is basically teaching our students how to learn and how to think on their own. Good readers do not read without thinking, comprehending and making meaning from text. How many times have you had a student ask you, "Why can't you just tell me the answer?" Unfortunately, with many answers available to this generation at the drop of a hat, via high-speed Internet, students often do not want to work out or search for an answer. Our job as educators is to make students *want* to think and discover. We finally get to bring creativity and collaboration back into our classrooms! The purpose of these chapters will be to help you and your students view reading and literacy as a type of learning and thinking and as a way for students to demonstrate their comprehension of content.

The second half of this book gets down to business. These chapters will include lessons, strategies and activities linked to Standards that can be easily implemented or adapted to meet the needs of 21st-century learners. The Common Core Standards emphasize the importance of evidence-based argumentation skills and inquiry-based thinking. These chapters will show you how to incorporate and use a variety of relevant types of texts in your classroom. They give you a strategy, called All A's for Everyone, that can be used when developing your own lessons by absorbing academic content; analyzing information, text and media; argument; and real-world application.

The closing chapters will focus on how to successfully balance the demands between teaching academic content and literacy, grading and planning. For the record, I strongly believe that, to develop competent college and career-ready students, we need to teach young people to be well-rounded. When I ask my 8th-grade students what they're interested in on the first day of school, many can't give me an answer. Of course, they often begin the year thinking that "I don't know" is an answer. Can they not articulate what they're interested in, or do they honestly not know? Those who can provide a vague answer, such as sports, video games or shopping, can't see the connection to who they are as a person or what those interests may mean for their futures. Content area knowledge should be a guide that helps students realize their personal interests and hopefully develop hobbies from them. A student once told me that when she graduated, she wanted to go to nursing school but later told me that she hated science and was planning to take only the necessary classes in high school. She didn't realize that science and nursing are closely related. How is that possible? Students are going through the motions of school without finding meaning. We need to engage them in meaningful ways that help them develop their interests and see the connections to their future.

The appendixes will offer readers lists of reproducibles and lists of sample activities aligned to the English Language Arts Common Core Standards for History/Social Studies and Science and Technical Subjects, Grades 6–12. I hope these tools will make this book easy to use and guide you toward implementing the Standards into your classroom. Remember: I hate change, but the strategies and activities provided here can be implemented either in full force or in small doses!

Examination of the Main Course

Before we get started, I want to take a minute and really get you to know the English Language Arts Common Core Standards for History/Social Studies and Science and Technical Subjects, Grades 6–12. Let's begin by examining exactly what the Standards are asking us to do and then analyze how the three grade bands progress from 6th to 12th grade. The best place to start is to look at the fundamentals of each Standard, which I refer to as "the meat," and then move on to how to apply the multistep higher-level thinking skills to each Standard. Think of this upping of the Standards as adding all the things that make a meal complete—side dishes, seasonings and, of course, dessert!

Why Does This Even Matter?

Now that we know what we're doing in History/Social Studies, let's talk about why the progression of skills is important in the Common Core. It is clear to see from Table 1.1 that the English Language Arts Common Core Standards for History/Social Studies Standards, Grade 6–12, build on one another from year to year. It's significant to note that the higher grade bands are not just incorporating more work or more skills; they're raising the level of analysis, questioning and thinking skills. Each Standard grows just like a child; it changes in small ways but evolves (with our help) for the better. This is fantastic for teachers because it serves as a ready-made tool to be used for differentiation and student growth. Regardless of the content being covered, we can take a student to a deeper level of learning through analysis and inquiry-based learning and thinking instead of simply moving on in a text or assigning a student more work.

Now let's take a look at the ELA Common Core Standards for Science and Technical Subjects, Grades 6–12 (see Table 1.2, pp. 8–10).

TABLE 1.1 Common Core Standards for History/Social Studies

Grades 6–8	Grades 9–10	Grades 11–12	Basically . . .
1. Cite specific textual evidence to support analysis of primary and secondary sources.	Cite specific textual evidence to support analysis of primary and secondary sources, attending to such features as the date and origin of the information.	Cite specific textual evidence to support analysis of primary and secondary sources, connecting insights gained from specific details to an understanding of the text as a whole.	"Because I said so" isn't good enough. Students need to understand how to back up their thoughts and opinions with text-based evidence. As they progress as learners, they should use this evidence to draw insightful conclusions and gain in understanding. Students should be able to identify and analyze primary and secondary sources.
2. Determine the central ideas or information of a primary or secondary source; provide an accurate summary of the source distinct from prior knowledge or opinions.	Determine the central ideas or information of a primary or secondary source; provide an accurate summary of how key events or ideas develop over the course of the text.	Determine the central ideas or information of a primary or secondary source; provide an accurate summary that makes clear the relationships among the key details and ideas.	A hyped-up version of main idea and summarizing. Students will begin by identifying central ideas and move on to summarizing without opinion, then to analysis of the way a text develops and comprehending relationships within a text.
3. Identify key steps in a text's description of a process related to history/social studies.	Analyze in detail a series of events described in a text; determine whether earlier events caused later ones or simply preceded them.	Evaluate various explanations for actions or events and determine which explanation best accords with textual evidence, acknowledging where the text leaves matters uncertain.	Text Structure: Chronological order, cause and effect, problem–solution and description. Students need to understand the way information is presented and the reason behind it.

(*Continued*)

TABLE 1.1 (Continued)

Grades 6–8	Grades 9–10	Grades 11–12	Basically . . .
4. Determine the meaning of words and phrases as they are used in a text, including vocabulary specific to domains related to history/social studies.	Determine the meaning of words and phrases as they are used in a text, including vocabulary describing political, social, or economic aspects of history/social science.	Determine the meaning of words and phrases as they are used in a text, including analyzing how an author uses and refines the meaning of a key term over the course of a text (e.g., how Madison defines *faction* in *Federalist* No. 10).	Figure out what a word or phrase means, and think about why the author chose to use it. How students find meaning in a word or phrase will determine how well they comprehend it.
5. Describe how a text presents information (e.g., sequentially, comparatively, causally).	Analyze how a text uses structure to emphasize key points or advance an explanation or analysis.	Analyze in detail how a complex primary source is structured, including how key sentences, paragraphs, and larger portions of the text contribute to the whole.	Author's writing style mixed with text structure. Students should be able to break down a text and see how structure impacts meaning.
6. Identify aspects of a text that reveal an author's point of view or purpose (e.g., loaded language, inclusion or avoidance of particular facts).	Compare the point of view of two or more authors for how they treat the same or similar topics, including which details they include and emphasize in their respective accounts.	Evaluate authors' differing points of view on the same historical event or issue by assessing the authors' claims, reasoning, and evidence.	Author's purpose, mixed with point of view. Students need to analyze the validity of various texts, compare numerous texts on the same subject and finally assess or argue for or against an author's claims or reasoning.

7. Integrate visual information (e.g., in charts, graphs, photographs, videos, or maps) with other information in print and digital texts.	Integrate quantitative or technical analysis (e.g., charts, research data) with qualitative analysis in print or digital text.	Integrate and evaluate multiple sources of information presented in diverse formats and media (e.g., visually, quantitatively, as well as in words) in order to address a question or solve a problem.	Get with it. Reading isn't just about words. Students will be able to incorporate a variety of visual, technical and quantitative analysis in print or digital text.
8. Distinguish among fact, opinion, and reasoned judgment in a text.	Assess the extent to which the reasoning and evidence in a text support the author's claims.	Evaluate an author's premises, claims, and evidence by corroborating or challenging them with other information.	"He said," "she said." Students will understand that it's OK to question a text. Yes, it is.
9. Analyze the relationship between a primary and secondary source on the same topic.	Compare and contrast treatments of the same topic in several primary and secondary sources.	Integrate information from diverse sources, both primary and secondary, into a coherent understanding of an idea or event, noting discrepancies among sources.	Don't take my word for it. Students will understand how information is presented differently in primary and secondary sources. They will use this information to develop an understanding of the content or topic.
10. By the end of grade 8, read and comprehend history/social studies texts in the grades text complexity band independently and proficiently.	By the end of grade 10, read and comprehend history/social studies texts in the grades 9–10 text complexity band independently and proficiently.	By the end of grade 12, read and comprehend history/social studies texts in the grades 11–CCR text complexity band independently and proficiently.	Students will have the necessary skills to learn on their own. Don't worry; you're not out of a job!

Source: Drawn from Common Core State Standards Initiative (2010).

TABLE 1.2 Common Core Standards for Science and Technical Subjects

Grades 6–8	Grades 9–10	Grades 11–12	Basically
1. Cite specific textual evidence to support analysis of science and technical texts.	Cite specific textual evidence to support analysis of science and technical texts, attending to the precise details of explanations or descriptions.	Cite specific textual evidence to support analysis of science and technical texts, attending to important distinctions the author makes and to any gaps or inconsistencies in the account.	Defend yourself! Use text-based evidence and analyze a text's validity and consistencies. Students should become reading critics.
2. Determine the central ideas or conclusions of a text; provide an accurate summary of the text distinct from prior knowledge or opinions.	Determine the central ideas or conclusions of a text; trace the text's explanation or depiction of a complex process, phenomenon, or concept; provide an accurate summary of the text.	Determine the central ideas or conclusions of a text; summarize complex concepts, processes, or information presented in a text by paraphrasing them in simpler but still accurate terms.	Main idea and summarizing, beefed up. Analyze a text's explanation of a process. Basically, don't be afraid to question a text. Students need to be able to decipher what's important; when summarizing a text, students must accurately present the material.
3. Follow precisely a multistep procedure when carrying out experiments, taking measurements, or performing technical tasks.	Follow precisely a multistep procedure when carrying out experiments, taking measurements, or performing technical tasks, attending to special cases or exceptions defined in the text.	Follow precisely a complex multistep procedure when carrying out experiments, taking measurements, or performing technical tasks; analyze the specific results based on explanations in the text.	Follow directions! Students will be able to complete a multistep procedure, realizing that small details are significant and finally analyze the results based on textual evidence.

4. Determine the meaning of symbols, key terms, and other domain-specific words and phrases as they are used in a specific scientific or technical context relevant to *grades 6–8 texts and topics*.	Determine the meaning of symbols, key terms, and other domain-specific words and phrases as they are used in a specific scientific or technical context relevant to *grades 9–10 texts and topics*.	Determine the meaning of symbols, key terms, and other domain-specific words and phrases as they are used in a specific scientific or technical context relevant to *grades 11–12 texts and topics*.	Figure out unknown words, phrases, symbols and key terms using a variety of tools.
5. Analyze the structure an author uses to organize a text, including how the major sections contribute to the whole and to an understanding of the topic.	Analyze the structure of the relationships among concepts in a text, including relationships among key terms (e.g., *force, friction, reaction force, energy*).	Analyze how the text structures information or ideas into categories or hierarchies, demonstrating understanding of the information or ideas.	Examine and analyze how a text is structured. Students should consider how information progresses, as well as cause-and-effect relationships.
6. Analyze the author's purpose in providing an explanation, describing a procedure, or discussing an experiment in a text.	Analyze the author's purpose in providing an explanation, describing a procedure, or discussing an experiment in a text, defining the question the author seeks to address.	Analyze the author's purpose in providing an explanation, describing a procedure, or discussing an experiment in a text, identifying important issues that remain unresolved.	Author's purpose: Students will be able to analyze why an author is writing and the author's intentions behind what they include and discuss. Eventually, students will be able to identify what the text or author has failed to answer.

(Continued)

TABLE 1.2 (Continued)

Grades 6–8	Grades 9–10	Grades 11–12	Basically
7. Integrate quantitative or technical information expressed in words in a text with a version of that information expressed visually (e.g., in a flowchart, diagram, model, graph, or table).	Translate quantitative or technical information expressed in words in a text into visual form (e.g., a table or chart) and translate information expressed visually or mathematically (e.g., in an equation) into words.	Integrate and evaluate multiple sources of information presented in diverse formats and media (e.g., quantitative data, video, multimedia) in order to address a question or solve a problem.	Turn words to pictures. Students will be able to take information expressed in words and translate it into a visual form and vice versa. Students will use multiple sources of information and media to answer questions and solve problems.
8. Distinguish among facts, reasoned judgment based on research findings, and speculation in a text.	Assess the extent to which the reasoning and evidence in a text support the author's claim or a recommendation for solving a scientific or technical problem.	Evaluate the hypotheses, data, analysis, and conclusions in a science or technical text, verifying the data when possible and corroborating or challenging conclusions with other sources of information.	Become a literary critic, in the information sense. Question an author's findings, claims, data and analysis. Verify information whenever possible.
9. Compare and contrast the information gained from experiments, simulations, video, or multimedia sources with that gained from reading a text on the same topic.	Compare and contrast findings presented in a text to those from other sources (including their own experiments), noting when the findings support or contradict previous explanations or accounts.	Synthesize information from a range of sources (e.g., texts, experiments, simulations) into a coherent understanding of a process, phenomenon, or concept, resolving conflicting information when possible	Students will begin by analyzing compare-and-contrast relationships from a variety of sources on the same topic. Eventually, students will be able to synthesize this information to understand the given content or topic.
10. By the end of grade 8, read and comprehend science/technical texts in the grades 6–8 text complexity band independently and proficiently.	By the end of grade 10, read and comprehend science/technical texts in the grades 9–10 text complexity band independently and proficiently.	By the end of grade 12, read and comprehend science/technical texts in the grades 11–CCR text complexity band independently and proficiently.	Students will be able to learn and use information without your holding their hand the whole time! They will understand grade-level content!

Source: Drawn from Common Core State Standards Initiative (2010).

Stepping Outside Your Department, Finding a Different Content Friend

I hope that, regardless of what subject you teach, you take some time to analyze and compare all of the Common Core Standards. You can easily see the similarities between the English Language Arts Common Core Standards for History/Social Studies and for Science and Technical Subjects. The possibilities for collaboration with the Common Core are endless! Remember, change is easier with a friend. Talk to your colleagues about what they're teaching and how they're teaching it. Too often, the teachers' lounge breeds negativity and sob stories. Make it a goal to find someone else ready for a little bit of spice! Collaboration is the key to success, not only for our students but for our teaching. I promise that you can learn at least 10 facts or skills from every teacher in your building. Take advantage of what's right in front of you. The Common Core Standards are not only content based; they enable teachers to implement a school-wide structure of inquiry-based, higher-level thinking and learning.

So, that was the so-called meat of the English Language Arts Common Core Standards for History/Social Studies and Science and Technical Subjects, Grades 6–12. The following chapters will get to the good stuff—the seasoning, sides and, my favorite, dessert! All of these Standards and their mastery will help your students become self-taught thinkers who are prepared for college and the demands of the 21st-century workforce. How you season your Standards is up to you, but that's the great news! Whether you like things spicy, salty or sweet is all in the presentation! As I've said, I'm not a big fan of change, but even I don't mind trying a new recipe now and then. Sometimes the results are surprisingly scrumptious!

References

Common Core State Standards Initiative. (2010). *Common core state standards for English language arts literacy in history/social studies, science, and technical subjects.* Washington, DC: National Governors Association Center for Best Practices and Council of Chief State School Officers. Retrieved March 5, 2013 from www.corestandards.org/assets/CCSSI_ELA%20Standards.pdf

Robb, L. (2003). *Teaching reading in social studies, science, and math: Practical ways to weave comprehension strategies into your content area teaching.* New York: Scholastic.

CHAPTER 2

Relax, You're Not Starting Over! Here's What You're Already Doing

Introduction: I'm Already Awesome

When I first became a parent, which hasn't been for long, I felt like I lost a little bit of my identity. Don't get me wrong, I love every minute of parenthood, but I had to learn to view myself differently, and so did the people around me. As a teacher, some days I truly wonder who I am or who I'm supposed to be. I don't mean this in some insane way, but more in the sense that, as a teacher, I just teach, right? Of course, you know what an absolutely crazy job that is in today's world. Every day I may be asked to be teacher, parent, evaluator, paper passer-outer, hall monitor, babysitter, house cleaner or disciplinarian—all before 3rd period. Your role as an educator is constantly changing, but you are a teacher! That's already impressive because you wear all these hats and many more! This chapter is going to focus on the good you're already doing in your classroom and how it can be easily aligned with the English Language Arts Common Core Standards for History/Social Studies or Science and Technical Subjects.

Every day you're doing great things in your classroom. You do have bad days, of course, but that doesn't mean it's time to throw in the towel! The Common Core Standards are not intended to show you everything you're doing wrong or even how to do things better. They are intended to make our students college and career ready for a world that is constantly changing. With rapid change, it's hard to ever feel caught up. However, the Common Core allows teachers to progressively adapt the tools they are already using to meet the demands expected of today's youth. The skills presented in the Common Core Standards give our students the tools they need to be collaborators, creators and problem solvers, all qualities that employers and—let's face it—educators are looking for in employees and students! Think about it: don't we really want the same things from our students that the Common Core is implementing?

Although I believe in the basic components of the Standards, I want to emphasize that this is a book about teaching. It contains no magic formulas for how to increase your test scores or make students come to school. I understand that assessment is critical for what and how we teach our students, but I am not an advocate for national high-stakes testing.

Allen (2000) said it best:

> It's important to remember that measuring your height doesn't make you grow any faster and weighing yourself doesn't make you lose weight. If we continue to let assessments that least inform classroom practice take a disproportionate amount of teaching and learning time, progress in the very areas the assessments supposedly measure will decrease from lack of high-quality instructional time. (p. 200)

Let's begin this chapter by looking at some of the strategies and activities you're already doing that make you a great teacher! Later, we'll examine how you can be even better! See Table 2.1.

TABLE 2.1 History/Social Studies Examples for Grades 6–8

Standard	What You're Already Doing
1. Cite specific textual evidence to support analysis of primary and secondary sources.	Are you asking why? Perhaps 500 times a day? That's great! Activities may include requiring students to defend their opinions, hopefully with fact, article critiques, completing Venn diagrams on information presented in primary and secondary sources and justifying an argument. Think about how many times you've used someone's first-hand account (diary, journal entries, letters) to supplement your textbook. See, you're awesome!
2. Determine the central ideas or conclusions of a text; provide an accurate summary of the text distinct from prior knowledge or opinions.	Helping students decipher key points, summarize information and distinguish the difference between their own thoughts and opinions and text-based information. This would include activities like writing a summary, KWL charts and discussions on what a student already knows about a given subject.
3. Identify key steps in a text's description of a process related to history/social studies.	Ensuring that students understand what made an event occur or the steps leading up to an event or through a process. This would include activities like timelines and flow charts.
4. Determine the meaning of words and phrases as they are used in a text, including vocabulary specific to domains related to history/social studies.	Vocabulary activities! Does your classroom contain lots of highlighting of key words, scanning the text, using context clues and coming up with definitions as a group? All of these activities are a great place to build from for vocabulary development for the Common Core! What about discussions on what causes vocabulary to change? History!

(Continued)

TABLE 2.1 (Continued)

Standard	What You're Already Doing
5. Describe how a text presents information (e.g., sequentially, comparatively, causally).	This may be a new one for some of you, and that's OK! Text structure has been long left in the English classroom, but guess what: it's back! Working with this Standard is as simple as having students select which graphic organizer is appropriate for the information given. Students decide whether a T-chart or timeline is better for a given text. I'm sure you've examined text structures many times, along with their impact on the meaning of a text; perhaps, it just wasn't your focus at the time!
6. Identify aspects of a text that reveal an author's point of view or purpose (e.g., loaded language, inclusion or avoidance of particular facts).	History and Social Studies teachers have this one in the bag! Questioning why the Bill of Rights was signed or what its authors were trying to accomplish? Check. Point of view and purpose are without a doubt built into teaching history. Try to go more than a day *without* including this Standard. Impossible! Activities could include journaling, role-playing, debating or literature reviews.
7. Integrate visual information (e.g., in charts, graphs, photographs, videos, or maps) with other information in print and digital texts.	Easy! This Standard would include activities like watching a movie clip, analyzing data, comparing photographs and videos or mapping an event. These activities can be easily integrated with any print or digital text that you're working on. Not only are they great resources, but they are fabulous for keeping students involved and attentive! I bet you're doing some of these daily!
8. Distinguish among fact, opinion, and reasoned judgment in a text.	This Standard can be easily integrated with a focus on primary and secondary sources. You're likely already having students decipher fact from opinion by using a wide variety of print and digital texts, having debates, role-playing and analyzing text validity.
9. Analyze the relationship between a primary and secondary source on the same topic.	Compare–contrast at its finest! Tools for this Standard would include T-charts, text-based scavenger hunts, Venn diagrams and research projects.
10. By the end of grade 8, read and comprehend history/social studies texts in the grades text complexity band independently and proficiently.	Getting students involved in the reading process, whether it's through questioning, class discussions, modeling or note taking. Students are reading every day!

Ask Not What You Can Do for the Common Core, But What the Common Core Can Do for You

The English Language Arts Common Core Standards for History/Social Studies enable teachers to build a curriculum that is thoughtful, integrative and inquiry based. The Common Core actually encourages educators to use more than a textbook! Think of the creativity that not only your students but you too can begin using in the classroom! The Common Core gives students the knowledge and tools to cite and analyze a variety of sources and gives teachers the opportunity to teach using a variety of means to help their students master academic content. It may take some time getting used to the numerous resources that can be used, but they will make teaching easier, in the sense that our students will be more involved using thought-provoking strategies for learning. One of the biggest changes in the History/Social Studies Standards is the variety of texts, both print and visual, that teachers will need to incorporate into their daily planning. What's important is that you're still teaching the same content, which is of great importance, but now you get to teach it in a manner to create well-rounded, college- and career-ready students. In Standards 1–10 for History/Social Studies, content still gets to be the star of the show, but now they have much better backup dancers!

Now let's take a look at what Science and Technical teachers are already doing to help their students be prepared for the 21st-century workforce. See Table 2.2.

TABLE 2.2 Science and Technical Subjects Examples for Grades 9–10

Grades 9–10	What You're Already Doing!
1. Cite specific textual evidence to support analysis of science and technical texts, attending to the precise details of explanations or descriptions.	Asking students to defend their answers and opinions. Activities would include using a text to support a scientific hypothesis, completing research papers, article critiques, debate, document analysis, fishbowl or projects and giving specific details to support analysis.
2. Determine the central ideas or conclusions of a text; trace the text's explanation or depiction of a complex process, phenomenon, or concept; provide an accurate summary of the text.	Encouraging students to figure out the main idea and intentions of a text and then to accurately summarize, including specific details. Students will be analytical readers in the sense that they can question how or why a text reaches its specific explanation. Activities you're probably already doing include summarizing, flowcharts and note taking.

(Continued)

TABLE 2.2 (Continued)

Grades 9–10	What You're Already Doing!
3. Follow precisely a complex multistep procedure when carrying out experiments, taking measurements, or performing technical tasks, attending to special cases or exceptions defined in the text.	This Standard is what science teachers work on every day. Asking students to follow and read directions *closely*! Activities you're already engaged in include labs, experiments, worksheets, journaling, demonstration, note taking, gathering information and data and actively participating in discussion and observations.
4. Determine the meaning of symbols, key terms, and other domain-specific words and phrases as they are used in a specific scientific or technical context relevant to *grades 9–10 texts and topics*.	Vocabulary! Whether you're teaching definitions, context clues or roots it will help students master this Standard. Activities include vocabulary definitions and comparisons, jeopardy games and creating keys and symbols.
5. Analyze the structure of the relationships among concepts in a text, including relationships among key terms (e.g., *force, friction, reaction force, energy*).	All things are related in science, right? This is a Standard you're using somehow every day, whether it's discussing the relationship between the atmosphere and climate or the structure of how an experiment is presented versus the same information from a textbook.
6. Analyze the author's purpose in providing an explanation, describing a procedure, or discussing an experiment in a text, defining the question the author seeks to address.	Teaching students to dig deeper into a text by asking what's the point? What's the author trying to do and why? Activities may include challenging lab or experiment results that are either against class members or world renowned, writing an essay on why an author's work was or is significant, critiquing articles or discussing how an experiment and a print account are related.
7. Translate quantitative or technical information expressed in words in a text into visual form (e.g., a table or chart) and translate information expressed visually or mathematically (e.g., in an equation) into words.	It's possible that this is my favorite Standard. Interesting visuals to demonstrate comprehension of information and vice versa? Yes, please. Activities for this Standard may include plotting scientific data onto various graphic organizers, charts or graphs. It may also include presenting information found in the visuals into a well written summary of significant information.

8. Assess the extent to which the reasoning and evidence in a text support the author's claim or a recommendation for solving a scientific or technical problem.	Students get to be the graders and potential scientists in this Standard! Activities you may already be using include answering questions about a reading, fishbowl circles, critiquing articles, analyzing the validity of labs and experiments and questioning how authors support their information. Inquiry-based projects on how to improve a theory and change it would also be included.
9. Compare and contrast findings presented in a text to those from other sources (including their own experiments), noting when the findings support or contradict previous explanations or accounts.	Hands on learning! Activities include completing labs, experiments, research, data collection, documentation, concept mapping and Venn diagrams.
10. By the end of grade 10, read and comprehend science/technical texts in the grades 9–10 text complexity band independently and proficiently.	Helping students develop strategies for reading comprehension to ensure that content can be mastered and students become independent thinkers and problem solvers! Activities include reading, taking notes, summarizing, developing theories and much, much more!

Keep Doing What You're Doing

Needless to say, class discussions, group work, projects, portfolios and numerous other tools are being used in your classrooms every day to ignite student interest in learning content. I encourage you to take the Standards for your specific content area and grade band and complete a sample chart of your own listing of the tools, strategies, activities and specific lessons you're already doing and that are aligned with the Common Core Standards. Blank sample charts for each grade band and content area can be found in Appendixes A1–A6 (pp. 125–135). Doing this will give you a starting point for determining what to keep doing and hopefully help you do what you're doing with more purpose. It is important that our intent is not lost in the translation to our students.

Schmoker (2011) begins his *Focus* book with a general question and answer that can make the big picture a little less complicated.

> What is essential for schools? Three simple things: reasonably coherent curriculum (what we teach); sound lessons (how we teach); and far more purposeful reading and writing in every discipline, or authentic literacy (integral to both what and how we teach). (p. 2)

Three things. That's pretty easy, right? I know that most days things seem complicated, and I understand the demands put on teachers today. However, maybe we should take a minute to reevaluate the big picture and our intentions and goals as teachers. What do we really want for our students? Years ago, while skimming my lesson plans, an administrator asked me, "Why do you include, 'Students pass the state achievement test' in your rationale for teaching every day?"

My response was easy: "Because I want them to pass the achievement test. That's the goal, isn't it? Everything is based on a score."

"Is that the reason you teach it?" he asked. It was awkward for a minute. I honestly wasn't sure whether I was being disciplined, we were making small talk, or he was actually curious about my answer. I'm not sure how long it took for me to come up with an answer, but it felt as though an hour had elapsed.

"I teach it because they [the students] need to know it," I stammered. Not a good answer, but I really didn't have a better one at the time. For some reason, he seemed to find this acceptable, and our conversation must have moved on. However, I have no idea what we talked about because I was still stuck on his question asking why I teach what I teach. When I left school that day, the encounter played over and over in my head. What should I have said? Why do I teach what I teach? I continued to think about it while brushing my teeth, feeding my cats, taking my shower and, of course, while driving to work the next morning. As you know, grading papers isn't the only type of schoolwork teachers bring home with them each night.

The next day during my planning period—I had to wait that long because teacher mornings are typically frantic—I marched (not tiptoeing this time) into my principal's office. "Why did you ask me that yesterday?" I asked. Clearly, he had no idea what I was talking about. He was really the master of wait time. Finally, I gave him a hint: "About wanting students to pass the achievement test?" I had lost sleep, been worried for 24 hours, and he didn't even remember our conversation.

"Oh, I was just wondering," he replied. "Your lesson plans were very specific, and I thought it was interesting that you included it." What? How do other people's lesson plans look? At that point in my then short teaching career, I had begun to believe that the only reason we taught anything was so that our students could pass a standardized test to help our district get much needed funding.

"Do you think I should be teaching something else? It was clearly aligned with a specific Standard and indicator." I was still fired up.

"Not at all," he responded. "I just think a state test alone is not a reason to teach something to a child. Is there any other reason they may need to know what they're learning in your class?" At that moment, the sun came out from behind the clouds, birds began to sing, and I realized just how fortunate I was to have this man as my boss.

With the support of my wonderful administrators, I began rethinking why I teach what I teach. I also promised myself that state testing would never again appear in my lesson plans. The new answer to his question became "because I want students to leave my classroom smarter and better than they were when they arrived. I want them to be prepared for their future and to become successful members of society." I hope that before you try to change what you're doing completely, you take some time, whether while brushing your teeth or planting a garden, to ask yourself what am I doing that's good? What has worked in my classroom? How have I been able to see my student's progress both academically and socially? The key is not to ask yourself what you like but rather what *works* for you and your students, which aren't always the same thing. Once you've truly reflected on what works for you and your students—the real success stories—keep doing what you're doing. As for the rest of it, get rid of it, or find a way to make it work!

Working with What You Have

Here's a little secret: not all teachers and schools have the same resources and tools. Trust me, if you are lacking resources, I understand. In a building with 600 students, we have two computer labs with 26 working computers each. Guess what: I find a way to make it work, and so does every fantastic teacher in my building. Is it ideal? No. Would I love to have an iPad for every student? *Absolutely!* I'm not implying in any way that if you do have SmartBoards in every room and a computer for every student, your job is any easier. If anything, working with technology and especially learning to use these high-tech tools is even more complicated and potentially more time-consuming.

It's true that the English Language Arts Common Core Standards for History/Social Studies and Science and Technical Subjects do involve the use of much more technology and media, but I'm here to tell you that, regardless of the tools you have, we can make it work. Technology needs to be integrated, of course, because that's what our students need to be college and career ready. If you have the technology you need, the upcoming chapters will give you ideas on how to use it to meet the demands of the Common Core through digital meaning, reading and writing. If you're school isn't quite 21st century yet, we'll improvise to make sure that all students have the tools they need to demonstrate proficiency of content.

I know firsthand that technology on its own can be a little scary to those who aren't tech savvy yet. I'm the type of person who tries to get her speakers working for 15 minutes before realizing they're not plugged in. Two or three times a week, I have to ask the teacher next door for help on the computer or a computer program. I admit it: technology frightens me, but I started off taking baby steps to make it work. Regardless of what I like and don't like, my students must have what they need to be prepared for the future. I'm not quite running full force, but I consider my progress along the lines of an uppity skip.

More good news on the Common Core is that neither technology nor the textbook has to be a leading star because of the huge variety of sources we're going to be using for teaching and learning. The Common Core creates an all-star cast, and you get to pick the lead roles for the various lessons you teach. If you have an experiment that you feel is beneficial to student growth, great! Pick some videos, opposing articles and research components to go along with the unit. If you think your textbook clearly and accurately portrays the events leading up to the American Revolution, fantastic! How about adding a movie clip showing a battle scene, a letter by John Adams, a webquest as a Loyalist or a piece of art? You don't have to have a billion things for students to read every day, but you do need to supplement your material enough that students are exposed to a variety of text and media types. Yes, art is text, but we'll argue about that in another chapter.

Preparing to Get Jiggy with It

At this point, I hope you've thought about the good work you're doing. In upcoming chapters, we'll examine how to take that work and make it better and eventually, in baby steps, add some new spices to our kitchen.

At the end of every school year, I throw away my lesson plan book. Well, really I recycle it. I am one of the few people in our current technological era who continue to plan with pencil and paper. I told you that I hate change. Recycling my plans doesn't mean that I teach the following school year with all brand-new, bright eyed ideas that keep every student engaged for every second of our 50-minute periods. Wouldn't that be nice? The goal of starting over is to analyze what worked and what didn't work.

Lesson plans and teaching components are not made of concrete. They have to be built to jiggle, like Jell-O.

I'm not saying you have to write an extensive three-page lesson plan every day. Instead, ask yourself, "Why am I teaching this? How will it help my students be prepared for the future? Is it aligned with the Common Core that is intended to give my students the skills they need to be contributing and successful members of the 21st century?" Then decide that the best way to present the knowledge to students is not by telling them but by making them think about it and figure it out on their own. This is a new concept for some of us, especially in a world where answers and feedback are expected almost immediately, thanks to our fast paced world.

Find a way to embed meaning and purpose in your lessons, while leaving room for a little jiggle. We can continue to teach what we're teaching, but we have to be prepared for some flexibility along the way. If you're teaching a unit on space that somehow leads to a meaningful conversation on how our environment is impacted by the atmosphere, be ready to roll with it. I know we want our kids to be on task and thinking about what we want them to think about, but isn't it a good thing if they can make connections and find meaning linked to content in other ways? I'm not saying to stop a lesson and talk about the previous night's episode of *Big Brother* but rather to allow students to inquire and use a TV show or some other outside-the-box vehicle as a learning tool or supplement to your content.

In the following chapters, I hope to make the jiggle in your lessons come a little bit more easily. For some, the jiggle may begin with a small sway, but as long as you're moving, that's success. The first thing we'll do is find a way to add or adapt what we're already doing to make it even better!

Review: What to Do, What to Do!

- Try not to feel overwhelmed by change.
- Keep doing what you're doing but with purpose.
- Complete the Standards charts with the lessons, strategies and activities you're already doing in your classroom (Appendixes A1–A6, pp. 125–135).
- Find the good in the Common Core.
- Examine your resources, texts and media tools, and then find more of them!
- Be prepared for student inquiry, encouraging higher-level text-based questions.

References

Allen, J. (2000). *Yellow brick roads: Shared and guided paths to independent reading.* Portland, ME: Stenhouse Publishers.

Common Core State Standards Initiative. (2010). *Common core state standards for English language arts literacy in history/social studies, science, and technical subjects.* Washington, DC: National Governors Association Center for Best Practices and Council of Chief State School Officers. Retrieved March 5, 2013 from www.corestandards.org/assets/CCSSI_ELA%20Standards.pdf

Schmoker, M. (2011). *Focus: Elevating the essentials to radically improve student learning.* Alexandria, VA: Association of Supervision and Curriculum Development.

CHAPTER

How to Make It Even Better—Yes, It's Possible

Introduction: Reflection as a Starting Point

I'm confident that reflection is the most important and worthwhile skill in teaching and learning. Maybe you keep a journal or reflect with your colleagues during planning. Maybe you rethink the events of your day on the way home or while brushing your teeth. Reflection may be something you're already doing, either without the purpose of improving your instruction or in order to see how you can grow as a teacher. I like to do all of the above! I think about my work constantly (even when I really don't want to), but I find it calming and helpful to keep a handwritten (yes, pen and paper) reflective journal of my school day. I may not write every day, but it's a tool for me to strengthen my skills and analyze things that may or may not have been successful, whether it's related to planning, instruction or classroom management. As Sousa (2011) states, "Teachers serve as valuable and authentic role models when they use creative and critical reflection to improve their practice" (p. 254).

What's important to remember is that reflection is not only the end; it's the beginning. Reflection is crucial in implementing the Common Core Standards into our classrooms because reflection is key in undergoing any type of change. The first thing we should ask ourselves is what we've learned or what we know that can make the process easier. For teachers, consider the following reflective questions:

- What works for me? How do I enjoy running my classroom?
- What works best for students? In which ways are they most productive?
- Is my classroom set up to be conducive to learning?
- What percentage of my class time is spent on teacher-centered lecture, collaboration, projects, worksheets and the like? Analyze the results, and think about how they impact student learning.

- How can I be better?
- What should I continue to do, and what shall I leave behind?

These are the big questions for teachers in preparing for their year. However, reflection can be found most valuable to educators when creating new lessons and materials. It's kind of like reflecting on your reflections. According to Allen (2000), "Assessing, evaluating and starting again are critical steps for students and teachers" (p. 227). This chapter will emphasize that new doesn't always mean change and that change doesn't always mean different. But sometimes it does. Through reflection and analysis, teachers can use the tools and lessons they have as a starting point when working with the English Language Arts Common Core Standards for History/Social Studies and Science and Technical Subjects. When looking at what you have and determining whether you can make it Common Core ready, consider the following reflective questions to guide you in your planning.

- Am I asking students to work together or collaborate? If not, how can I adapt this lesson to make sure students are discussing what they're learning?
- Are my students thinking in order to discover an answer, or am I giving it to them? If not, how can I adapt my approach to make students think? Where is the inquiry?
- Has this lesson been successful in the past? Were students engaged in learning? Did they see a connection to the world?
- Were students asked to use various texts as evidence of their learning or opinions? What texts can I integrate into this lesson or unit?
- Were students given the opportunity to be thoughtful? How can I make this lesson more inquiry based and less teacher centered?

If you're like me, you probably have a few lessons that can be, unfortunately, trashed. Through reflection, I found that my number one problem was giving students the answers. What a terrible trait for a teacher! I thought that by telling them information, they would remember it. I was having them apply the information after I gave it to them myself, when I should have been giving them the opportunity to find the information. Oh, if it were only so simple. If you have some lessons to trash, don't be discouraged. When my husband and I were first married, I thought it would be nice to cook him a special meal for his birthday. I spent hours preparing gorgonzola mashed potatoes, fried chicken, corn casserole and a black raspberry chocolate torte. I have to say, dinner was perfect. The chicken was crunchy, not raw in the center, which was my main concern, the mashed potatoes light and fluffy and the corn casserole scrumptious! My husband loved it. I was feeling good as I presented the chocolate torte; it looked delicious and sophisticated. All seemed well even as I was cutting it. Then we tasted it. Imagine cough syrup in cake form but worse. My husband ate as much as he could and faked a full belly instead of finishing it. I was devastated and pouting on the couch as he cleaned up. When he came in, he asked what I was so upset about. The chicken was perfect, the corn casserole scrumptious and the potatoes delicious. Who cares about dessert? He was right, it wasn't all as perfect as I had planned, but overall it was pretty darn good! Don't get hung up on the negatives; celebrate the positives.

My point is not about my cooking skills but rather that these are tough questions. The good news is that you probably have a gazillion lessons and materials that you can use to get started with your work with the Common Core. This chapter is intended to get you thinking about what you do every day and what you ask your students to do every day. It will discuss taking what you already have and do and making it better. We will examine why teaching with purpose is important to student learning, how to develop thinking students versus tell-me-the-answer students, why group work matters, why projects and unit planning are important. Let's get to it!

Turning Basic to Brilliant: Higher-Level Thinking

In my opinion, worksheets get a bad rap. I'm not saying that they're the answer to our problems, but, man, sometimes I feel as though, if I make a copy, I'm dooming my students to failure. Worksheets are like anything else in our profession: if they get our kids thinking, they're probably not that terrible. Do I recommend passing out copies from a workbook every day? Absolutely not. Do I think that you can adapt and create handouts that can get students collaborating and analyzing texts, leading to inquiry-based projects and discussions? *Yes!*

I begin our discussion on adapting materials to meet the higher-level thinking skills necessary to master the Common Core Standards with worksheets because, let's face it, we all use them at some point. It may be in a form of a summative or formative assessment, a vocabulary activity, directions for a lab or identifying symbols on a map, but we use them. And, by golly, if they're done well, there's nothing to feel bad about.

The first step in worksheet improvement is looking at the verb. Now, I understand that we want students to be able to identify, explain and define the numerous concepts we teach. However, I think that this knowledge can be demonstrated through higher-level questioning if a student is proving comprehension of content, not just a word or event. If you really aren't ready to totally give up the identify-and-define question, that's OK. Baby steps, remember? What I would recommend is at least adding a follow-up question. If you want students to identify one cause and one effect of the Civil War, go with it, but then ask a follow-up question to get them using or applying the knowledge. For example, discuss how the war would be different if slavery hadn't existed. Consider the examples in Figure 3.1

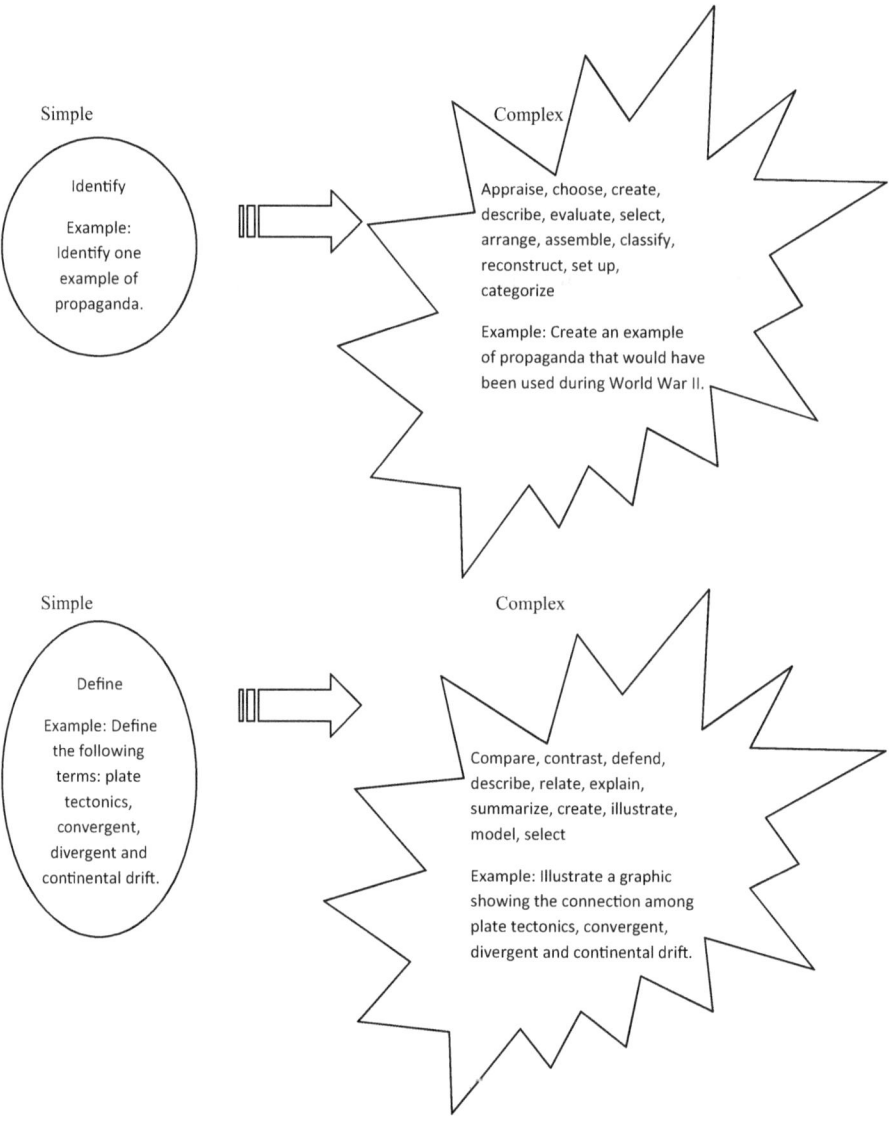

FIGURE 3.1 Verb Switching

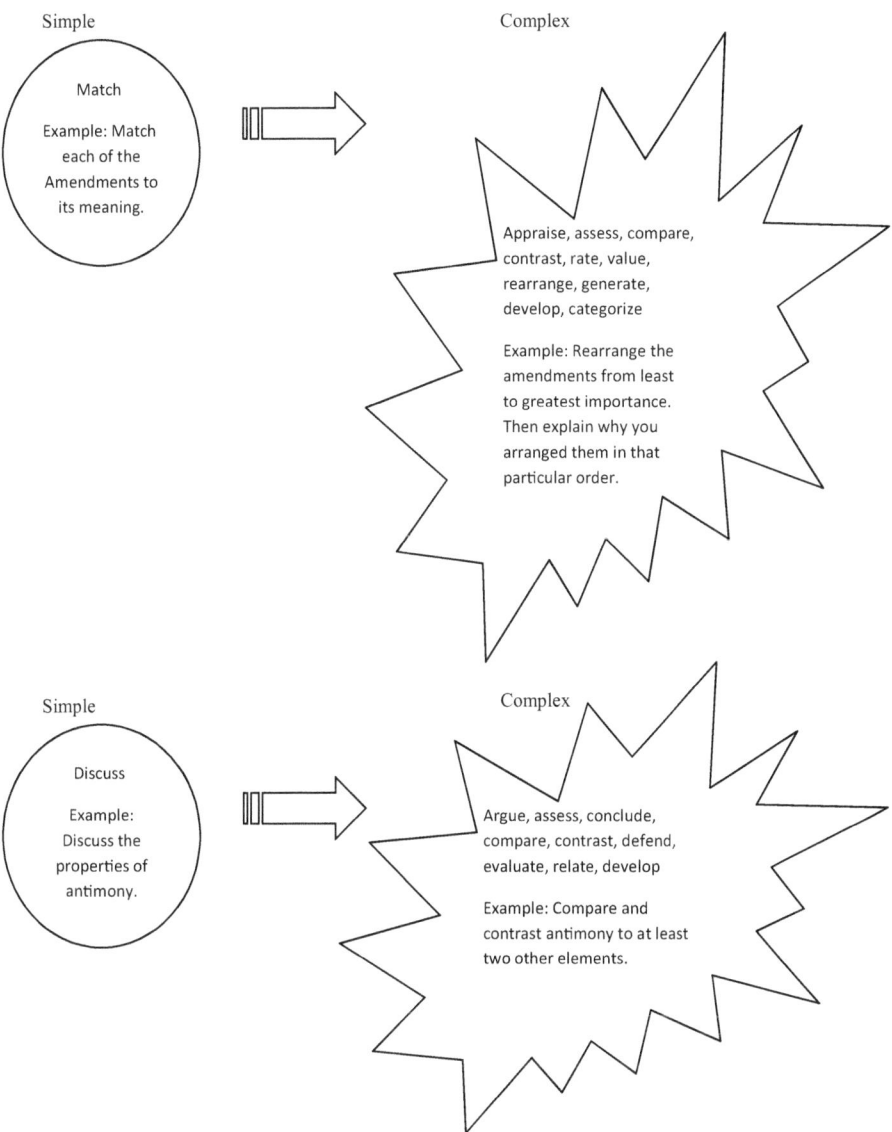

FIGURE 3.1 (Continued)

when you're trying to change your verbs quickly without changing the meaning or intention of your question. This can also be found in Appendix A7 (p. 137).

Anyone can take a look at one of the numerous Blooms' Taxonomy charts available online and change a question, but what is important to working teachers is that the question's intentions aren't lost in translation. It wouldn't make sense for me to change the verb "identify" to "argue" because the intention of the question has changed. However, if I'm asking students to appraise, they must be able to identify. If you want a student to identify, you don't have to change the question's intentions to meet the higher-level thinking skills. The examples in Figure 3.1 show how your intentions can stay the same while getting students to think more critically about the content.

Worksheets aren't the only way to quickly improve students' critical thinking skills. It took me years to master the concept of wait time in my classroom. Why would discussion be any different? As Allen (2000) states:

> When we look at the way teachers and students interact in a typical experience with the text, we often find teachers asking lots of questions (often prepared in advance or found in guides) as a way of checking for students' understanding or extending the content of the text. These kinds of questions might be called product-oriented. (p. 81)

I needed to know whether my students were completing their reading, but I was asking in a way that only made them recite information, not think. We talk a lot in my room, but through reflecting, I found that I was asking students questions like, "Why do you think that?" "What's that mean?" Or just "why?" It's good to ask why, but I had to change how I asked questions or held discussions with students. According to Robb (2003) discussions should "invite students to formulate their own questions and connections, think using what they have read as foundation, listen to others, then shape their emerging ideas into talk that transforms what they feel and think" (p. 254). Effective discussion cannot be productive without the use of higher-level thinking and skills.

The first thing I tried was investing in a pair of dice that had higher-level thinking verbs on them, such as "analyze," "predict," "justify," but it was distracting to me and my students, especially if we were right in the middle of something. So I had to think about what I could do in my classroom that would help me ask critical questions without throwing off the focus. I already use the Popsicle method, whereby you draw students' names on Popsicle sticks randomly from a jar to ensure that everyone is participating. So what's one more jar? I decided to add a variety of higher-level verbs to 25 Popsicle sticks, and we were in business. Now, this solution may not be convenient for you, but if so, think about what you do naturally. Do you carry around a clipboard? Maybe it would be easier for you just to copy the verbs and carry them with you? Maybe you want to use two different verbs every day of the week? What's important is that you find what works for you!

The final strategy for turning basic into brilliant is hands-on time. Hands-on time is giving students the time they need to create, design and construct. Giving students the opportunity to apply what they're learning doesn't have to be with pencil and paper or discussion. Let's get them thinking creatively! I'm not talking about having students color diagrams or cut and paste all day, but what if we asked them to create models of how the ocean floor shifted during a recent tsunami or to illustrate the battle zones of the Civil War, a soldier's travels or the change between isotopes? Not only do hands-on projects teach our students to think creatively and critically, they help us keep them engaged. Engaged and learning at the same time? Super! Be careful, though; sometimes we're so worried about getting kids engaged or making sure things are fun that we lose sight of our learning goals. Teaching is really a balancing act that we do every day for our students!

Group Work Galore: Letting Students Talk

Here's another secret. I know this is a book for teachers, not my diary, but here's a confession: I hate group work. (I dislike only one other thing more—projects—and we'll get to that later.) I like the idea of group work, but, oh, how it causes me to worry! Is one person doing all the work? Are the students on task? How can I fairly and accurately grade group work? How will I monitor all the group members at one time? Will things get out of control? What if my principal comes into the room and thinks we're having a party instead of preparing for a debate on the American Revolution? Here's the thing: at some point you have to ask yourself, as I did, what's best for the students? What do they need to be successful? Without a doubt, they crucially need the skills to work in a group and to collaborate with others. Even better, students benefit in many ways from working in groups. According to Atwell (1998), "Learning is more likely to happen when students like what they are doing. Learning is also more likely when students can be involved and active and when they can learn from and with other students" (p. 69).

The Common Core Standards call for collaboration among teachers, students and the community. What's the reason for this shift? Collaboration is a *must* for college and career readiness. As Gallagher (2004) states, "I have to remind myself that the adolescents sitting in front of me may be struggling mightily, and then I remember how important a role of collaboration can play in raising their levels of comprehension" (p. 105). Effective grouping and group work can help students at any level improve their understanding of content. Group work may consist of students collaborating in pairs or groups of two to five. In my opinion, any more than five students are too many.

If you're working in groups and students are talking with each other every day, fantastic! I don't mean talking the first or last five minutes of class; I mean being engaged in a heartfelt debate or analysis of a newly learned topic. Group work isn't meant for everything, but it can be beneficial to student learning in the right context. Eyster and Martin (2010) maintain that "if you are going to use small group interactions to advance learning objectives, make sure that this is the best design to reach your goals" (p. 192). If you're letting students talk about content, see whether you can do anything to improve the discussions and get students talking with purpose. Gallagher (2004) states that "giving students the opportunity for group discussion prompts them to confront their confusion and teaches them that they are responsible for making their own meaning" (p. 123). If you are not a fan of group work, like me, let's take a few baby steps before we start to run. Tables 3.1 and 3.2 show several Standards and examples of how to get started with group learning in your classroom. Table 3.1 deals with the English Language Arts Common Core Standards for History/Social Studies Standards, Grades 6–8, and Table 3.2 deals with the Standards for Science and Technical Subjects, Grades 11–12.

My final advice on group work is to ask someone else. Experts are all around you. Don't be afraid to visit other teachers in your building and invite them to visit your classroom when you're doing something great. If you really want to find ways to make what you're doing better and linked to the Common Core, work as a team. Talking with other teachers about what you're planning to do or what you've already done gives you ideas for the future and improves the quality of your teaching. A brilliant teacher once told me not to go out and try to recreate the wheel. The people who know your student population best surround you; don't be afraid of taking some of the ideas out of their toolbox.

Projects: Why They Keep Us Awake at Night and How to Finally Get Some Shut-Eye!

Projects. Sigh. Group projects. *Arrggh!* Are projects more work for me or more work for my students? How will I ever be able to get them all graded? Should my students work in groups or on their own? How much class time

TABLE 3.1 ELA Common Core Standards for History/Social Studies Standards, Grades 6–8

Grades 6–8	Possible Ideas for Student Collaboration
1. Cite specific textual evidence to support analysis of primary and secondary sources.	• Pass out a variety of primary and secondary sources on any topic. In partners, have one student highlight all the opinionated/bias information in pink. Ask the other student to highlight all the factual information in yellow. When they're finished, ask them to discuss which details would best support a given idea and why. Then have them present the information to the class. • Debates! Let students develop an opinion and find the textual evidence to back them. If you want to make it really challenging, ask students to play devil's advocate and debate for the side they disagree with.
2. Determine the central ideas or conclusions of a text; provide an accurate summary of the text distinct from prior knowledge or opinions.	• Ask students to read any passage or short piece of work; if you're using a textbook, maybe one section but no more than 2–3 pages. Have students close their books and write a 8- to 10-sentence summary of what they've read. When they're finished, they should cut each sentence into a strip and trade strips with a friend. (It's best if they have separated each sentence for easy cutting.) Each student will then go back to the text and identify where each idea was presented by writing the paragraph number or sentence on the back of the strip. Students can work together to prove where they found the information or whether the summary does not accurately portray the text. Great close reading activity!
3. Identify key steps in a text's description of a process related to History/Social Studies.	• Put students in groups of 4–10, depending on how many steps are in the content you're teaching. Give each student a piece of paper with a specific step written on it. Tell students they have three minutes to line up in the correct order of the process, whether it's how a bill becomes a law or what led up to the American Revolution. • Allow students to create a digital storyboard to represent their comprehension of the content.

(*Continued*)

TABLE 3.1 (Continued)

Grades 6–8	Possible Ideas for Student Collaboration
4. Determine the meaning of words and phrases as they are used in a text, including vocabulary specific to domains related to history/social studies.	• Put each vocabulary word from a unit or chapter on an index card. You'd need one for each student in your class. Tape an index card to each student's back. They can ask four people for hints on their word. Once they guess it correctly, they can take their card. This gets the students thinking of how to give hints without giving away the answer and helps students develop a sense of words in content.
5. Describe how a text presents information (e.g., sequentially, comparatively, causally).	• Split students into groups of 4–5. Have each group write on the topic you're covering with a different purpose. For example, if you're covering the Civil War, have one group write in chronological order, one in terms of cause and effect, another in compare–contrast or descriptive. Have the groups present the information to the rest of the class, and discuss how and why they are different.
6. Identify aspects of a text that reveal an author's point of view or purpose (e.g., loaded language, inclusion or avoidance of particular facts).	• In small groups, have students research a topic connected to what you're covering in class. Tell students they must find at least four sources, one being a newspaper article, one a letter, journal or editorial and two from any other nonfiction sources of their choice. Along with their research paper, ask students to turn in a reflection of how each source presented the information differently, identifying the author's purpose. • Assign students to write on the same topic from different points of view. For example, if you're covering the American Revolution, have students write as slaves, Thomas Jefferson, a Loyalist, a patriot or a British soldier. Once students are finished writing, create groups, each one with a point of view represented, and have students discuss the similarities and differences.

7. Integrate visual information (e.g., in charts, graphs, photographs, videos, or maps) with other information in print and digital texts.

- In small groups, assign (or if you're feeling relaxed, allow students to choose) one form of visual information to create representing the topic being covered. They must find or create five visuals that represent the content. This could include a scene from a movie, a commercial, charts, graphs, photographs, digital videos, maps or storyboards.
- In partners or groups of three, ask students to create digital storyboards of what they've learned on a particular topic.

8. Distinguish among fact, opinion, and reasoned judgment in a text.

- Have students work with one partner to highlight a text. I think newspaper articles, letters and speeches work best for this standard. One student should highlight everything in the text that is fact in blue, the other should highlight anything opinionated in yellow. Once they're finished, they should analyze the information and see what could be considered reasoned judgment and why.

9. Analyze the relationship between a primary and secondary source on the same topic.

- Piece of the pie: Give each group one primary and one secondary source on the same topic to analyze, take notes on and discuss the relationship. Once they are finished, ask students to present their information to the class. As each group is presenting, the other groups should add the information to their pie to see how the pieces fit together.

10. By the end of grade 8, read and comprehend history/social studies texts in the grades text complexity band independently and proficiently.

- Peer tutoring, jigsaw reading/learning, group projects and many more!

TABLE 3.2 ELA Common Core Standards for Science and Technical Subjects, Grades 11–12

Grades 11–12	Possible Ideas for Student Collaboration
1. Cite specific textual evidence to support analysis of science and technical texts, attending to important distinctions the author makes and to any gaps or inconsistencies in the account.	• Split your class into 4–6 groups depending on class size. Give each group one text on the same topic to closely analyze. Have each group present their analysis to the class citing 5–10 details from the text. Once all groups have presented, allow students to rank the texts from best to least based on most valid information, inconsistencies and research. This could take 1–3 class periods.
2. Determine the central ideas or conclusions of a text; summarize complex concepts, processes, or information presented in a text by paraphrasing them in simpler but still accurate terms.	• Have every student complete the same reading for this activity. When they are finished, have them complete domino note cards with a well written summary. Domino note cards are similar to playing dominos; each card will hold two events or details from the text. Each student should complete an accurate summary with 5–10 cards, depending on the length of the text. Once finished, the students will find a partner. Tell students to mix up their dominos and to have their partner figure out the correct order of the concept, process or information. When both students have correctly completed the dominos, they must use the information to agree on one central idea or conclusion from the text.
3. Follow precisely a complex multistep procedure when carrying out experiments, taking measurements, or performing technical tasks; analyze the specific results based on explanations in the text.	• In groups of 3–5, ask students to create a demonstrative video of how to correctly carry out a procedure or specific lab. Each group should be assigned a different procedure or lab to be taught to the rest of the class. • Have students work in small groups to complete labs, experiments or other technical tasks. • Ask students to complete a similar experiment with one variation in each group. Once they are finished, reorganize the groups so that there is one member remaining in each of the previous groups. Have the new groups analyze the similarities and differences. Ask students to cite the text as to why the results were the same or varied.

4. Determine the meaning of symbols, key terms, and other domain-specific words and phrases as they are used in a specific scientific or technical context relevant to *grades 11–12 texts and topics*.	• Role-playing isn't just for literature. Ask students to create or become a vocabulary word for a class period to help their peers comprehend and remember the word or phrase's meaning. Once words are assigned, give students the option to dress up, model or act out a scene represents the word or phrase. • Working in pairs or groups of three, assign each group 1–5 words. If working with words, students must create a symbol for each word and write a paragraph defending and explaining their choice for a symbol. Have the groups share out and argue who has the best symbol based on their reasoning.
5. Analyze how the text structures information or ideas into categories or hierarchies, demonstrating understanding of the information or ideas.	• Give each group a large piece of chart paper and markers. After they complete the assigned reading, ask them to select one graphic organizer to create and display the information, based on the structure of the text. If you're class is familiar with graphic organizers, let them pick one their own; if not, you may want to give them 4–5 to chose from.
6. Analyze the author's purpose in providing an explanation, describing a procedure, or discussing an experiment in a text, identifying important issues that remain unresolved.	• Fight the author: In this activity, each group will be assigned a text (article, textbook, newspaper) to examine some type of research or experiment. After completing the reading, each group will analyze the author's purpose for the research or lab. Then the groups will look for holes in the author's research or presentation of information. They will essentially complete a critical review of the author's work and create a plan for improving on it.
7. Integrate and evaluate multiple sources of information presented in diverse formats and media (e.g., quantitative data, video, multimedia) in order to address a question or solve a problem.	• Ask groups of 3–4 to create a research paper and presentation for their class. You will have to allow up to a week or two for students to complete this activity and have access to a computer lab, iPads or laptops. Assign or allow students to select a topic. Tell students they must complete research on their topic and cite at least five sources in a bibliography. Their presentation must include at least three types of media, one of which was originally created by the group themselves. • Near the end of a unit, once students are well informed on a given topic, present them with 5–10 sources including quantitative data, video and multimedia on the topic. Working in groups, have students evaluate each source, ranking them from weakest to strongest based on their ability to address the question or solve a problem.

(Continued)

TABLE 3.2 (Continued)

Grades 11–12	Possible Ideas for Student Collaboration
8. Evaluate the hypotheses, data, analysis, and conclusions in a science or technical text, verifying the data when possible and corroborating or challenging conclusions with other sources of information.	• Debate the scientist! You get to play too. In small groups, give students the opportunity to research a specific experiment or scientific finding, using multiple sources. Students should evaluate the information and cross-reference whenever possible. Their presentation of information will be set up as a debate. Either they can debate another group, or if you're feeling up to it, you can play the scientist and defend your work. Trust me, students love telling teachers how they're wrong.
9. Synthesize information from a range of sources (e.g., texts, experiments, simulations) into a coherent understanding of a process, phenomenon, or concept, resolving conflicting information when possible.	• Research projects work well here as well. I like to have students find and compare information, without my simply telling them where to look in the book. • Assign each group a sample of 2–4 texts to work with and analyze information. The following day, have each group rotate one member (jigsaw format) to share the information and bring other groups' information back. Groups should then synthesize the information for a class discussion.
10. By the end of grade 12, read and comprehend science/technical texts in the grades 11–CCR text complexity band independently and proficiently.	• Ask students to complete a given reading. Assign one group to make predictions, one to summarize, one to make connections, one to compare and contrast the information and one to ask questions. Have each group share out with the rest of the class. • We'll talk more about reading and comprehension in the next chapter.

will I have to sacrifice for them to be completed? Should they all complete the same project or have choices? That's what's scary about projects. We don't have answers, and—let's face it—teachers *love* answers. Maybe you think they'll take three days, and at the end of three days, you're students aren't even close to being finished. Uh-oh. Projects force us to be flexible, and flexibility is good, right? Better yet, projects teach our students to complete multistep procedures and think for themselves.

Whether you complete one project or five in a year, you're helping your students prepare for the future. Colleges and the workforce are now, more than ever, project focused, giving students and staff multistep directions and deadlines. The rest is often left to them to figure out. Projects teach problem solving and creative thinking, two of the Common Core Standards' fundamental skills. When I first started using projects in my classroom, I felt as though I was busier than ever. Not a second went by when I wasn't being pulled in every direction. Then I caught myself complaining to a colleague, "They need help with everything!" I went on ranting, "I spend all day answering questions that they [my students] should be able to find the answers to! We're working in the computer lab, for goodness' sake!"

As soon as I heard myself say that, I knew what the response would be. "Then why are you telling them the answers?" Well, I wasn't quite sure; I guess it was just easier. The next day we had what I like now to refer to as "I-don't-know day." This is a response we often receive from students, or maybe that's just me. The following day, when we were working again on our projects in the computer lab, my only answer to project questions was, "I don't know." And guess what? If I refused to tell them, they would figure it out, with the help of either the computer or a classmate. One boy said to me, "You have to help me. You're the teacher!"

"If you need help, of course I'd be glad to help you," I responded. "Do you need help with what you're learning? Do you not understand something? Or do you want me to tell you the answer?" This sweet child rolled his eyes at me, turned around and put his headphones back on. Guess what? He found the answer . . . *on his own* . Once your students are familiar with working on projects and having the freedom and tools to work on their own, life is grand. We are a security blanket for our students and that's OK, but we have to give them the confidence to take risks and explore through learning on their own. Projects give students that freedom and power. It's a strange feeling when students don't need you every second to answer questions and you can have real conversations about what students are doing and learning through their projects.

Another assumption about projects is that you need to chunk out one or two solid weeks to work on projects every day, get them completed, turned in and graded. Why? What if every Friday were Project Day? You can continue to teach your content, perform labs and complete assignments while a project is ongoing. That's what's great about projects: they are multistep assignments. Students can work at their own pace, and the content of your teaching can go right along with what students are learning through inquiry-based projects. Projects don't have to be the center of your classroom; if you're not ready for that, you can use projects to supplement what you're already doing. Projects help students stay engaged, and by having options, they are proud of their work and can teach their peers.

Units: Why They're Important to the Common Core

I get made fun of a lot. I'm a compulsive planner and proud of it. Other teachers get a glimpse of my lesson plan book during a staff meeting or common planning time and see that I have—let's call it—a vague idea of what I'm doing three weeks down the line. They're shocked. "You know what you're doing next week? I barely know what I'm doing tomorrow!" OK, I get that; we're all busy. But it's not as though I just sit around all day planning lessons, and I understand that my students may not work at the pace I have planned. However, I know ahead of time where I want them to go, as well as the purpose of what and how I am teaching. Unit planning also allows me to monitor what I have and have not covered and how to tie it all together to deepen student comprehension. Wiggins and McTighe (2005) assert that "teachers are designers. An essential act of our profession is the crafting of our curriculum and learning experiences to meet specified purposes" (p. 13). Let's talk about why planning in units before planning one day at a time can be beneficial to students and teachers when working with the Common Core Standards.

We've all had days when we show up to first period with our lesson plan on a Post-it note or had to throw a lesson out the window and free-fall through a class period. It happens to the best of us, but it's definitely not ideal. Unit planning can take what you're already doing and tie your lessons together to make them powerful, connected and, most importantly, purposeful. A unit plan doesn't have to list every detail of every day; it's a general plan of what and how you're going to cover one or more Standards.

I'm not a fan of 10-page lesson plans, but you need to consider some significant factors. Most typical units should last 2–3 weeks to ensure that you are not trying to focus on too much at one time. If you have what you consider a unit that lasts 8–12 weeks, I would encourage you to break that unit into 3–4 smaller units to help you sharpen the focus for a shorter time span. If you're talking about a 12-week plan, you're really getting into curriculum development versus unit planning. In the course of one day, most teachers hit on at least 3–4 Standards in some form or fashion by breaking down units into smaller sections. With focused unit plans, we may still hit on several Standards, but instead of trying to cover everything, we know where our focus lies. Gallagher (2004) believes that "instead of trying to assess whether our students understand every layer of a complex work, we would better serve them if we consider the one or two areas within the text we think to be the most important and target those areas for our students' consideration" (p. 210). The unit plan format in Figure 3.2 offers a few things to consider when planning. A blank unit planning sheet can be found in Appendix A8 (p. 139).

Each part of the unit plan in Figure 3.2 has a specific purpose linked to the English Language Arts Common Core Standards.

- *Focus ELA Standards:* Select no more than three English Language Arts Standards for History/Social Studies or Science and Technical Subjects to focus on in one unit. It is inevitable that at times, you will be working with or teaching other Standards, but your focus will return to the selected ones. If you're hitting on more than one Standard, remember that you don't have to cram everything together. What you're teaching now will make a great connection to what you teach in the future.
- *Content focus:* You should try to be as specific as possible without getting down to daily plans. If you're teaching about the Civil Rights Movement, exactly what time period will you cover? How many years? Will you talk about specific people? If so, list them. What vocabulary will students need? Consider causes and effects and what you want students to take away from the unit.
- *Writing activities:* Writing is a way for students to demonstrate their understanding of content. Writing is also another form of learning. What assignments will you be giving that enable students to demonstrate knowledge through writing? This could include journals, essays, research papers, debate notes, summaries and more.
- *Reading activities—Primary and secondary sources:* Reading activities are split into primary and secondary sources because the Common Core is aiming to develop well-rounded students who know how to utilize a

Focus ELA Standards (no more than 3 or 4)	Content Focus	
Writing Activities	Reading Activities	
	Primary	Secondary
Speaking and Listening/Collaboration Opportunites	Projects	

FIGURE 3.2 Unit Plan

Multimedia/Visual Information	Assessments	
	Formative	Summative
	◯	◯
Possible Enrichment	Critical Thinking Questions	

FIGURE 3.2 (Continued)

variety of materials. Think specifically of how you will be using various lab reports, graphs, charts, personal accounts, letters, scholarly journals, online resources, maps and other sources to be integrated with your content. Will students be using these materials for research, comparison essays, comprehension, analysis of content or making connections? Every reading and text should serve a specific purpose.

- *Speaking and listening/collaboration opportunities:* What types of opportunities will you be creating to ensure that every student has the chance to speak and listen? The goal would be that students have this opportunity *every* day! Will you be including small- and large-group discussions? Pair shares? Individual or group presentations? Lab groups?
- *Projects:* A project every three weeks may sound like a lot to some of you, but remember that you're still in charge. You get to decide the extent of what you're doing. Projects are simply multistep and, hopefully,

inquiry-based, learning. Whether they're individual or group, two days or two weeks, they are essential to student success in the future.

- *Multimedia/visual information:* Learning isn't just about lectures and a textbook anymore. What media and tools are you going to expose your students to that will deepen their knowledge of the content? Consider the movie clips, graphs, photos and other vehicles that you would show to help students understand the time period and importance of the Civil Rights Movement. How will your students read the information?

- *Formative and summative assessments:* Formative assessments will show you exactly how you need to spend your time and when your students are ready to move on. This can be accomplished through thumbs-up, thumbs-down, observation, homework, class discussion and more. Summative assessment asks how specifically you are going to have students display mastery of the unit content. I encourage you to have at least 2–3 summative assessments for each unit to gather a bigger picture of what the student has mastered. Remember, summative assessments do not have to be formal paper–and–pencil tests.

- *Possible enrichment:* The Common Core forces teachers to be a little more flexible as we work to make learning student centered. That being said, things can get a little messy. Students will not be in the same place all the time. Enrichment is not meant to be busy work. Enrichment is made up of opportunities for students to learn more on their own, enriching the content that they're already learning. In working on the Civil Rights Movement, possible unit enrichment activities could include reading a fictional book on the subject, watching a movie on the subject, completing a project, writing an essay, researching a specific person or creating a timeline of events.

- *Critical thinking questions:* Planning ahead with higher-level questions that go along with your unit help you get a look at the big picture and prepare you to make your students think. If a question is prepared ahead of time, you are much more likely to ask it during a discussion than a question from the textbook. What questions will you ask that make your students think? These will be questions that you can continuously go back to throughout your unit.

Unit planning is crucial to improving what you're already teaching and using it to implement the English Language Arts Common Core Standards for History/Social Studies or Science and Technical Standards, Grades 6–12. The preceding format will get you thinking of the bigger picture and give you a purpose aligned with the Standards to make your students college and career ready. Plus, taking a few minutes to develop a short unit plan will make your daily planning much easier.

Review: What to Do, What to Do!

- Use reflection as a starting point. Examine what you know to be good and make it better. Toss out what doesn't work.
- Teach students to think critically by incorporating higher-level thinking questions and skills.
- Make group work work for you.
- Make students work to find answers.
- Provide students with the opportunity to learn through inquiry-based projects. Remember that projects can be used as a supplement to learning content or as a class-centered learning tool. The choice is yours.
- Take the time to plan small units. Unit planning will help you focus on specific Standards and provide you and your students with a distinct purpose.

References

Allen, J. (2000). *Yellow brick roads: Shared and guided paths to independent reading.* Portland, ME: Stenhouse Publishers.

Atwell, N. (1998). *In the middle: New understandings about writing, reading, and learning* (2nd ed.). Portsmouth, NH: Heinemann.

Common Core State Standards Initiative. (2010). *Common core state standards for English language arts literacy in history/social studies, science, and technical subjects.* Washington, DC: National Governors Association Center for Best Practices and Council of Chief State School Officers. Retrieved March 5, 2013 from www.corestandards.org/assets/CCSSI_ELA%20Standards.pdf

Eyster, R. H., and Martin, C. (2010). *Successful classroom management.* Naperville, IL: Sourcebooks.

Gallagher, K. (2004). *Deeper reading: Comprehending Challenging Texts, 4–12.* Portland, ME: Stenhouse Publishers.

Robb, L. (2003). *Teaching reading in social studies, science, and math: Practical ways to weave comprehension strategies into your content area teaching.* New York: Scholastic.

Sousa, D. A. (2011). *How the brain learns* (4th ed.). Thousand Oaks, CA: Corwin.

Wiggins, G., and McTighe, J. (2005). *Understanding by design* (2nd ed.). Alexandria, VA: Association for Supervision and Curriculum Development.

CHAPTER 4

Why Am I Teaching Middle and High School Students How to Read?

Introduction: Learning to Read or Reading to Learn?

You may think that reading is straightforward, that either you can read or you can't read. Oh, if only it were that simple! I'm sure you've sat through a staff meeting or two about teaching reading where everyone present was a reading teacher. Don't get me wrong—it's true—you're not necessarily teaching students *how* to read; you're teaching them how to *understand* what they read and how to *learn* through reading. Reading must be presented as an active task. Atwell (1998) states, "My students know I have reasons for any task I assign them and that I'll explain how I believe the assignment serves their purposes—as young adults, as their parents' children, as citizens, writers, readers, historians, and thinking human beings" (p. 23). This chapter will focus not on teaching our students how to read but on teaching our students how to *learn* through reading. Reading should always be assigned as an active process.

Have you ever had students miss a question on a text because they didn't understand what it was asking and then, once you explained the question, answered correctly? In our classrooms, we have the luxury of being able to help our students when they're confused, but what about on standardized tests? Do students have to miss a question if they don't understand what it's asking? What if we spent time in our classrooms teaching students to read and understand questions? Would this benefit them? Absolutely!

Gallagher (2009) states in *Readicide* that we must "surround academic texts with high-interest, authentic real-world reading" (p. 117). Isn't that how we learn as adults? Luckily, the ELA Common Core Standards for History/Social Studies and Science and Technical Subjects give us the power to do just that in our classrooms. Students are exposed to such a wide variety of texts and real-world reading that they will be prepared for college and career when they graduate. We learn the details of contracts, how to get places, how to make things, how to cook things and how to read more thoroughly. This chapter will walk you through helping your students understand how to read with the purpose of learning strategies to use before, during and after reading in order to promote learning. This chapter will also address our love/hate relationship with textbooks and how to effectively use them (or not) in your classroom. Finally, we will discuss how the English Language Arts Common Core Standards for History/Social Studies and Science and Technical Subjects can make differentiating a breeze.

Reading with Purpose

Do you ever really think about how you read? Or do you just sit down and do it? Most likely, you read a lot of different ways depending on your purpose. Personally, when reading a novel, I admit that I may skip over a part or two or even look ahead to the last page to find out the ending. If I don't understand something or recognize a location, I don't usually bother to look it up unless I need to know it in order to understand the story. I read before bed and am sometimes so tired that I have to look back a few pages the next time I pick the book up. Is this ideal reading for learning? I think not. How about directions? I read every single detail before I begin a project or recipe and then reference them several times during my work. My husband skims them before he begins and has to start over three or four times. OK, sometimes only once. He focuses on the model or figure of what he is creating, and I focus only on the words.

Unfortunately, I was always one of those kids who skip over all of the graphics in my textbook. I had no idea they held so much information because I wasn't taught to read them! I assumed that, because they included pictures, graphs and other "fun stuff," they were not important to the content and definitely would not be on a test. As literate adults, we read differently for different purposes, and we switch reading gears without ever thinking about it, like an automatic transmission. However, most of our students are manual shifters, if they bother to shift gears at all.

In content area classes, we are asking our students to read for information. Let's consider how reading for information is different from reading for pleasure, which is often how students have been taught to read, including looking for things like character and setting. The differences are quite significant. See Figure 4.1.

There are many differences in reading for pleasure versus reading for information, but several skills should carry over from one category to the other and can fit in both. Regardless of what students are reading, they

Reading for Pleasure/Literacy	Reading for Information/Learning
– Conflict	– Headings, Subheadings, Titles
– Characters	– Print Features
– Theme	– Graphics matter
– Action	– Sidebars, Pictures, Charts
– Entertaining	– Examples
– Setting	– Real People
– Chronological Order	– Texts are presented in various structures including chronological compare-contrast and cause-effect
– Tells a story	
– Details are not that important	
– If you miss something, you can usually still figure out what's going on.	– Details are important
	– Not presented as a story
	– May not be as high-interest
– High-interest	– Students have attached a negative stigmatism to non-fiction

FIGURE 4.1 Reading Purpose

need to be able to cite evidence, determine themes or central ideas, summarize, figure out unknown words, identify and analyze point of views and author's purpose and analyze the relationships among various texts. All of the above are required by the Common Core Standards. What a great opportunity for collaboration across content areas! Once students have been taught and have practiced how to read with purpose or to read for knowledge, they will gradually begin shifting gears naturally. Until they reach that point, we need to make sure students are reading with the intended purpose of learning and remind them how to shift gears.

When students are being taught to read for learning, they should be thinking about a few key strategies and be asking themselves a few basic questions. We'll talk about the strategies later in the chapter, but first let's discuss what our students need to understand to learn through reading. I like to hand out a bookmark similar to the one in Figure 4.2 when working with a nonfiction text.

If students know that they are reading to learn, they should be ready to shift into the gear of essentially searching for new and relevant information. I tell my kids it's like a treasure hunt for knowledge. The students with the most information win, usually an A. Is that a little corny for 8th graders? Yes, but if they're laughing at me, at least they're engaged! If students are taught to read for the purpose of learning, I like them to look at things, such as bold words, subheadings, graphics and the like, as hints or clues to finding the jackpot, which is the central idea of the text.

> My Purpose is to Learn _____.
> What do I already know about this topic?
> If my purpose is to learn, I need to consider the items below while reading.
> - Titles, heading and subheadings   − Bold or italicized print
> - Graphics, Pictures, Charts, Sidebars − People, Dates
> - Main Ideas/Important information   − Themes

FIGURE 4.2 Bookmark

Have students ever asked you, "Why do we have to read this?" or, as in my classroom, "Why are we *always* reading?" Tell them the purpose is to *learn*. Of course that's an extremely vague answer, but regardless of what you're teaching, that's why we read!

Reading is not a time filler; it's a learning action and should be presented as a task or process. Now, as professionals we know that not every student learns best by reading, but that's why we're here to expose them to a variety of tools, models, visuals and more to enhance their learning. Consider how we can deepen student understanding by teaching them to take away the most from the tools we are providing for learning. Acknowledging that students are completing a task when reading to learn, rather than reading without purpose, helps them understand that they are going to have a completed product once finished, the product being information and knowledge. The next steps will be how to apply what they've learned.

Before We Read, Let's . . .

As Allen (2000) states, "In reading education the importance of activating and building background knowledge has long been established as critical to the reading process" (p. 129). Sometimes, it's OK for students to just dive right into their reading, especially if they've already been exposed to the content. However, if they're not ready to shift gears, they may stall out, and once that happens, it can be difficult to get them started back up. I think highly of my students, and I have high expectations for them within and outside my classroom. At times, my expectations have been so high that I end up feeling disappointed, sometimes in my students, sometimes in myself. Through reflection, I've wondered what I did wrong or why my students couldn't perform a specific task or answer a certain question. It seems that part of the problem are my own assumptions. I have repeatedly believed that my students already know things, have previously learned tools or strategies or have read similar materials. At least, I thought they *should* know it, which led to misguided assumptions. And, let's face it, unless information and skills are repeatedly used and applied, our students lose them. Why was I becoming so upset that my students didn't remember information they learned three years ago? To meet the demands of the English Language Arts Common Core Standards for History/Social Studies and Science and Technical Subjects, students should think about several components before they begin reading to learn.

One question students should ask themselves before reading a text is what type of material will we be reading? A journal? Textbook? Article? Picture? Data? Can I tell whether this is a primary or secondary source? Once the sources are distinguished, students can consider how the text is set up and scan it for hints about what they're going to be learning. Most students look ahead in a text only to see how many pages they have to read! Students need to be clear on the purpose of their reading. Robb (2003) states that "setting a purpose directs students as they read, by helping establish guidelines for how to approach the reading and what information is essential" (p. 40). We need to encourage students to look for information that will make the text easier to read and understand. For lower readers, scanning the text ahead of time can be extremely helpful to student comprehension. It will enable them to have an idea of where the information is leading and to see how events are connected.

When scanning a text, students should be instructed on what to look for and be given a few minutes in class to see that it is an actual task. Before students begin reading, have a quick one- to two-minute discussion or pair share about what the students are thinking after the scan. A huge assumption that I made in my classroom was that students know to look at headings and subheadings. To my great horror, I came to find that often, just as they do with pictures, charts and sidebars, students skip right over headings while reading! As a prereading activity, ask your students to outline the chapter looking at only the headings. Then, either while they're reading or after they've finished, they can add information. This is a great strategy to help students get a visual of how a text is organized and how the headings flow together for an overview of the chapter.

I was floored that my students were ignoring headings and subheadings. I was even more shocked that they were ignoring graphics within their text. What gave my students the impression that graphics and headings weren't important? After a formative reading assessment, I found that nearly 70% of my students could not tell me any information from the given passage that could have been easily found in the sidebar! One student actually said to me, "I didn't know we had to read that part." Maybe it seems obvious to you that when you assign a reading, you mean everything in the text, but are you *sure* that your students see it the same way? Do they really understand the importance of the many graphics included in a text? And, as teachers, are we using the graphics, sidebars and other supplemental materials in a text to the best of our ability? Are we teaching our students that the information is not important? The answer may surprise you!

Teach your students that the graphics are not just a supplement to what they're learning in the text, that the information in the graphics is part of what they should be learning and that, through analyzing and understanding the graphics, the concept being presented will come much more easily. According to Fontichiaro (2010), "Sometimes, looking at an image gives us answers. Other times, we think of new questions to research" (p. 10). It's amazing how much interest can be raised by looking at a simple image related to the content. Fontichiaro recommends asking four questions when looking at images:

1. Who are the people in the image?
2. Are there any symbols?
3. What might those symbols mean? How do you know?
4. Can you draw any conclusions or inferences from the observations you made earlier? (p. 12)

Using graphics and images not only helps students understand and make connections with content, it gives them the skills necessary to make inferences about content.

Before reading, students can preview the vocabulary, along with the graphics and headings. Bold or italicized words are something that most students have been trained to look for from a very young age in preparation for vocabulary quizzes. Looking at the vocabulary words gives students another clue about the text. After completing a scan of the chapter, give your students some time to talk as a class or in pairs. Remember, talking is another form of learning. This gives students time to make connections, predictions and inferences and to hear the ideas of a peer that they may not have had during scanning.

While We Read, Let's . . .

In school, the majority of the magic seems to happen in our classrooms after students have completed a reading. I encourage you to have students interact with the text while they're reading or rereading. Not only does it keep your students engaged and on task, the text itself will become much more meaningful. The Common Core Standards want students who can *use* and *apply* the text in a variety of ways, not just as a stepping-stone to their teacher's lecture. Students need to be reading to learn. Table 4.1 lists strategies for learning while students are reading.

TABLE 4.1 Strategies to Use During Reading

Grades 9–10 ELA History/Social Studies Standards	Learning *While* Reading!
1. Cite specific textual evidence to support analysis of primary and secondary sources, attending to such features as the date and origin of the information.	• Highlight what's important. • Take notes. • Use sticky notes and flags. • Make a timeline of events. • Create a flowchart. • List facts versus opinions.
2. Determine the central ideas or information of a primary or secondary source; provide an accurate summary of how key events or ideas develop over the course of the text.	• Guided notes • Timeline of events • SQ3R • Create a tree diagram. • Hierarchy chart • Summary shout (Pick one student to start with the first thing that happened, allow him or her to pick the next student, who will give a second detail, and so on until you've reached the end of the text.)
3. Analyze in detail a series of events described in a text; determine whether earlier events caused later ones or simply preceded them.	• Annotated timeline • Annotated flowchart • Double-entry journal • Cause-and-effect graphic organizer • Domino chart • Stop and talk (Set a timer for every 5–6 minutes for students to discuss and analyze the text.) • Write from a different point of view.
4. Determine the meaning of words and phrases as they are used in a text, including vocabulary describing political, social, or economic aspects of history/social science.	• Find a synonym for each vocabulary word. • Explain how the word relates to the content without giving the definition. • Give the context clue that helped you figure out the word. • Create a visual representation of words or phrases. • Use vocabulary words or phrases as the headings for guided notes. • Circle unknown words.

Grades 9–10 ELA History/Social Studies Standards	Learning *While* Reading!
5. Analyze how a text uses structure to emphasize key points or advance an explanation or analysis.	• Flowcharts • Tell students they must represent the information from the text in a graphic organizer of their choice. After a few minutes of reading, discuss which organizers would or would not work based on the text.
6. Compare the point of view of two or more authors for how they treat the same or similar topics, including which details they include and emphasize in their respective accounts.	• Side-by-side readings • Venn diagrams • Double-entry journals • Stop and talk (Put students in pairs and give each one a different reading; every few minutes, have them stop and talk to compare and analyze the texts.) • T-chart
7. Integrate quantitative or technical analysis (e.g., charts, research data) with qualitative analysis in print or digital text.	• Concept drawing • Add a graphic (Ask students to supplement the text with a graphic every three paragraphs, two pages—whatever—depending on the length of the text.)
8. Assess the extent to which the reasoning and evidence in a text support the author's claims.	• Flowchart • Cluster diagram • Tree organizer • Hierarchy chart • Fact/opinion graphic organizer • Credible source vote (As the students go along in their reading, stop every few minutes to ask them to vote on whether they would consider the given text a credible source. Have them defend their answers.)
9. Compare and contrast treatments of the same topic in several primary and secondary sources.	• Venn diagrams • Up and add (Label and hang large chart paper around your room with the titles of various primary and secondary sources. As students are reading, allow them to get up and add sticky notes to any of the chart papers with what they consider to be relevant information.)
10. By the end of grade 10, read and comprehend history/social studies texts in the grades 9–10 text complexity band independently and proficiently.	• Have students read aloud. • Have students read silently. • Have students read for homework. • Have students read often. • Have students read for *learning*.

Most of these strategies work with any grade level and any content area, as long as the students are reading with purpose. What's really crucial is that we give our students the opportunity to learn through reading every day. Other teachers have said to me, "You're so lucky! You get to have your students read every day. That must be so nice!" I guess they assume I'm playing solitaire or coloring instead of grading the stacks of essays and papers on my desk? My point is that I'm not sure why content area teachers are under the impression that students shouldn't be reading every day in their classrooms. Have we given in to the idea that our students must be happy, entertained and out of their seats working every minute of every class period—only to sacrifice their own learning? It's important that students are engaged, but it's much more important that they learn how to be engaged with a text, whether it's words, media or any other type of visual.

Are we so tired of hearing our students complain about reading that we're giving them a one-page handout of notes instead of teaching them to read for the deeper meaning of the content? If so, don't give up! Try the strategies in Table 4.1, and make students see that knowledge is worth working for. We don't need to tell them the answers. You don't have to jump up and have students reading every day. Start with a day or two a week, find an article related to what you're teaching, but somehow, whether through baby steps, skipping or catapulting right in, get your students reading to learn! Fight their resistance—and, trust me, there will be resistance—and eventually they will give in to the work of learning. When they do, I promise you that it will be worth every second of the fight.

After We Read, Let's . . .

Generally, this is when the majority of teachers have students use what they've learned from their reading. Again, I encourage you to try to do a little more while your students are reading to keep them fully engaged in the text and to promote a deeper understanding of the content. Robb (2003) reminds us that "sometimes, simply rereading a sentence, paragraph, or page can put learners back on the comprehension track" (p. 150). Don't forget that some students may not be "done" with reading after the first time. Students comprehend at different paces.

The Common Core Standards are all about how students actually apply and demonstrate their knowledge, hopefully using practical, real-world skills. Many of the strategies for use during reading can be used after reading as well and vice versa. Table 4.2 shows some strategies to use after reading that will complement the Common Core.

TABLE 4.2 Strategies to Use After Reading

Science and Technical Subjects Grades 6–8	**After We Read, We *apply*!**

1. Cite specific textual evidence to support analysis of science and technical texts.	• Debate! Have students create note cards or digital notes in preparation.
	• Get students in the habit of citing the text by requiring them to begin sentences with one or more of the following stems:
	  – According to the text . . .
	  – The author said . . .
	  – On page xx, it said . . .
	  – From the reading I know . . .
	• Highlight the text after reading.
	• Written response essays
	• He Said, She Said (Picture Simon Says, but using textual evidence versus opinion or prior knowledge.)

2. Determine the central ideas or conclusions of a text; provide an accurate summary of the text distinct from prior knowledge or opinions.	• Write a summary. • Create a presentation. • Storyboards • PowerPoint or Prezi • Comic strip or poster • Graphic organizers • Create a brochure. • Reread and discuss.
3. Follow precisely a multistep procedure when carrying out experiments, taking measurements, or performing technical tasks.	• Perform a lab. • Give directions to another student. • Create a video demonstrating a procedure.
4. Determine the meaning of symbols, key terms, and other domain-specific words and phrases as they are used in a specific scientific or technical context relevant to *grades 6–8 texts and topics*.	• Use a dictionary, thesaurus or other source to define a word. • Use context clues to figure out unknown words or phrases. • Compare different meanings or uses for a word. • Create a visual to demonstrate the meaning of a word or phrase.

(Continued)

TABLE 4.2 (Continued)

Science and Technical Subjects Grades 6–8	After We Read, We *apply*!
5. Analyze the structure an author uses to organize a text, including how the major sections contribute to the whole and to an understanding of the topic.	• Complete a flowchart or other graphic organizer. • Ask students to create a puzzle with the information for a class member to complete. • Create an outline. • Chunk information. • Summarize. • Ask students to try to present the information using a different text structure.
6. Analyze the author's purpose in providing an explanation, describing a procedure, or discussing an experiment in a text.	• Argue with the author (through role-playing or debate). • Create a double-entry journal, but the right side is the *why* of the writing. • Write a critique of the text. • Role playing/author interview
7. Integrate quantitative or technical information expressed in words in a text with a version of that information expressed visually.	• Create a video. • Turn the text to a visual; create graphs, charts, video, brochures, drawings, story maps, cartoons, video games, movie clips, models, diagrams or art.
8. Distinguish among facts, reasoned judgment based on research findings, and speculation in a text.	• Graphic organizers • Debate • Role-playing • Rereading • Discussion • Identification games (Identify each sentence as fact, reasoned judgment or speculation.) • Categorizing
9. Compare and contrast the information gained from experiments, simulations, video, or multimedia sources with that gained from reading a text on the same topic.	• Graphic organizers • Jigsaw groups • Presentations using different sources of information • Fishbowl • Double reading
10. By the end of grade 8, read and comprehend science/technical texts in the grades 6–8 text complexity band independently and proficiently.	• Rereading • Discussion • Writing • Group work • Projects • *More reading!*

As I've explained, many of these activities can be used during or after reading and can be used in any content area. In my opinion, after reading is when we spend most of our time in the classroom. With the shift to the Common Core Standards, we should think about reading continuously or of reading as a process or as a piece of the learning puzzle. Our students shouldn't really ever be "done" with a text. If you're having a discussion about the content, students should have their texts out and readily available to cite. If you're completing a lab, they should be continuously examining directions or comparing findings. Hopefully, many, many texts should be the stars of our lesson. Using a variety of texts encourages your students to make comparisons and improve the odds that each student will find something that sparks their interest or makes them enjoy reading. Students who don't like reading their textbook may love to read real-world articles; struggling readers may love the opportunity to analyze visual texts and relate them to the content. This brings us to the idea of how best to use or incorporate textbooks into Common Core learning.

"I Love My Textbook!" Said No Student Ever

Textbooks. Personally, I have a love/hate relationship with them. We break up; we get back together. It's a never ending cycle. It's no one's fault that it doesn't work. We both just need more in our relationship. As a teacher, there are so many wonderful things about using a textbook: they usually come with supplemental materials, including tests, worksheets and discussion questions; the information flows in a logical order; all of the information can be found in one place; many offer online versions; our students are comfortable (through years of practice) with using them in class; and we trust the information to be reliable. These are all reasons for me to love using a textbook. Sounds great, right?

On the other hand, I'm forced to break up with my textbook often, and for good reason. Textbooks have a bad reputation. If we're reading from a textbook, before we've even gotten started, the moaning begins. You know what I'm talking about: students lugging their textbooks out as if it weighs 300 pounds; the groans and sighs; "This is boring!"; not to mention that half of the class left their books in their lockers or have lost them for the year. It's unfortunate, but this is the way we've taught our students to view their textbooks. We've used textbooks for the boring reading or for answer–the–questions activities, and then the fun comes afterward. We need to bring the fun to the reading. Luckily, we can do a few things to rekindle our student's relationship with their textbook.

The Common Core insists that we use a wide variety of sources. Most textbooks include a broad range of visuals and examples of texts, but it's difficult for students to understand the distinction and importance of multiple sources when, to them, they're all coming from the same source. Make your textbook *part* of your curriculum, not your curriculum itself for the year. According to Schmoker (2011), "much of a good education consists, as it always has, of a simple combination of one or more good texts matched with an interesting question" (p. 36). Students need more to keep them engaged. At this point, I usually hear how districts don't have money to buy extra texts, how teachers don't have time to find so many sources or how teachers don't have the materials they need to be successful. I understand. No one is saying that it's easy, but the materials are available, for free, and with time and practice, using multiple sources becomes easier and easier.

If you want students to find some love for their textbooks, start by presenting them differently. At the beginning of the year, wrap them up as presents and pass them out as gifts, or have students spend time creating their own meaningful book cover that represents the subject content. Explain to students that their textbooks are gifts because they are one of their most credible and easily accessible sources for learning, researching and completing projects throughout the year. They will be their go-to source for information. If you want students to like their textbook, spend some time making sure they understand it. Use some of the before-reading strategies, and compare the textbook with other texts or materials to show students that their textbook really is quite user-friendly.

If you want students to find some value in their textbooks, try taking them away from them more often. After an assigned reading, don't allow students to use their textbooks to find an answer: force them to use a different source (a map, a visual, the Internet, another book) to demonstrate understanding. They can check their answers later with the text and compare the two or more sources of information. Do your students use the textbooks for vocabulary? Show them the sentences from the book with the vocabulary words blocked out, and make them use the context clues to figure out possible words, events or phrases. In a short time, you'll hear, "Can't we just use our textbooks? It would be so much easier?" Well, it's not supposed to be so easy; it's supposed to make them think!

Textbooks don't have to be viewed as boring. Let textbooks be used for exploration, not just for sit-down-and–read-the-chapter type of learning. Here are some other suggestions:

- Present the textbook as a treasure of information, and then give students the chance to explore it for answers. Do you want your students to learn about the Underground Railroad? Tell them that and maybe three or four other things that you'd like them to know, and let them explore. Don't even tell them the page numbers. Get them to use their book and learn on their own.
- Ask students to create visuals to supplement or represent sections of their reading. Have students read different sections of the text and teach them to the rest of the class.
- Have students read only the visuals, sidebars and "extras" in their textbook without any of the actual text.
- Challenge students to summarize a chapter with only a 10- to 12-block comic strip.
- Create a brochure of the chapter.
- Turn a chapter into a picture book for younger learners. Students have to consider how the information will be presented differently.
- Create a lab, based on information or research found in the textbook.
- Act out a scene from the textbook.
- Let student's flag textbooks, or highlight and mark up digital textbooks.
- Be sure your students are given the chance to discuss what they're reading and connect ideas from the textbook to their own world.

Students are still going to ask you if they have to bring their textbook every day. Students are still going to "accidentally" forget their textbooks in their lockers. These are just things we have to deal with, but we can do our best to present the textbook as a gift for learning. Make using the text a privilege, not a punishment.

Common Core: Making Differentiating Easy

Our students are different. We know this. They read, write and learn in different fashions and at different speeds. Through differentiation, teachers try to meet the needs of every student. When all the students are doing the same thing and using the same texts and materials, differentiation can be tough and often becomes more modification than differentiation. Despite my good intentions when it comes to doing what's best for my students, but, with so many students at so many levels, sometimes I've thrown my hands in the air, ready to give up hope and feeling defeated. I know I need to help my students as individuals, but at times that can feel a bit overwhelming.

The English Language Arts Common Core Standards for History/Social Studies and Science and Technical Subjects allow enough flexibility for teachers to provide learning options, resources, texts, projects and strategies for a variety of learners. According to Tomlinson (2000):

> Teachers can differentiate at least four classroom elements based on student readiness, interest, or learning profile: (1) content—what the student needs to learn or how the student will get access to the information; (2) process—activities in which the student engages in order to make sense of or master the content; (3) products—culminating projects that ask the student to rehearse, apply, and extend what he or she has learning in a unit; and (4) learning environment—the way the classroom works and feels.

Let's use those same four elements to examine why the Common Core makes the process of differentiation easy.

The first element is content; this is the heart of the information or what we want the student to learn. The Common Core standards require students to use a variety of materials to analyze, compare and contrast. Why not have different students reading texts at various levels? The ELA Common Core Standards for History/Social Studies and Science and Technical Subjects ask that students be able to present and analyze a variety of digital and visual materials. Have some students learn through video and others through art, graphics or written text, depending on the need of individual groups of students, and then have them discuss the relationships as a whole. The Common Core encourages students to view texts in a wide variety of ways, enabling you to present reading to students at many different levels without singling students out or changing the content.

Process is how the student makes meaning of material. The Common Core Standards are broad enough that we can choose to present information to our students via a wide array of means and use the tools and strategies that work best with our own individual strengths. The Common Core encourages students to learn as an ongoing process by having students continuously cite, analyze, argue and use a variety of texts. No more reading and just moving on. Students will be asked to look at how information is organized and closely consider the steps they themselves or someone else must go through in lab work or to get a desired result. Teachers will be able to easily break down mastering each standard into steps for students to work through at their own pace. Students will practice working through multistep procedures, labs and technical tasks. The inquiry of the standards will enable students to find topics, projects and texts that they find interesting in order to keep them engaged in the learning process.

Products are the creation element of differentiated instruction, where we get to see how students can demonstrate their comprehension of content. By incorporating inquiry-based projects into your curriculum, students will be differentiating without your adapting anything at all. You will be encouraging learning and differentiation by providing your students with choices and teaching them the skills to learn and explore on their own. The days of handholding are over! Give your students the confidence to try new things, to explore and to take command of their learning. Students will be asked to create products like summaries, but it is up to you whether that will be through a presentation, digital storyboard, Prezi or written report. As long as you are asking your students to create to demonstrate knowledge, you will be differentiating.

We create the learning environment for our students, and we should consider a number of factors. The Common Core Standards will challenge you and your students, but that's how we learn. Struggle is good. It is up to you as a teacher to guide your students toward the knowledge without giving them the answers when things get tough. We have to be patient and teach patience. If our students feel safe and are encouraged to try new things, knowing that they may or may not work out, then the students are in an environment to learn. Will there be good and bad days? Of course, that's just part of the ride. The Common Core will not restrain you, it will encourage you to teach with materials you never dreamed possible and allow you to give individual students the materials and strategies they need for learning.

Review: What to Do, What to Do!

- Read with a distinguished purpose for learning. Present reading as a task.
- Prepare students for reading.
- Make reading strategies part of your instruction.
- Have students become engaged with the text while their learning. What are they doing while they're reading?
- Students aren't "done" when they stop their reading. They may not be directly using the text, but force them to refer to it and demonstrate understanding of the content.

- Don't try to make reading easy. Summarizing the chapter for your students is not the answer. Students learn with just the right amount of struggle.
- Make sure your students see the connection from their reading to how you're having them apply their knowledge.
- Remember, the textbook is not your curriculum. It's a tool for teaching. Do your best to make it fun!
- Use the Common Core to meet the needs of different learners.

References

Allen, J. (2000). *Yellow brick roads: Shared and guided paths to independent reading.* Portland, ME: Stenhouse Publishers.

Atwell, N. (1998). *In the middle: New understandings about writing, reading, and learning* (2nd ed.). Portsmouth, NH: Heinemann.

Common Core State Standards Initiative. (2010). *Common core state standards for English language arts literacy in history/social studies, science, and technical subjects.* Washington, DC: National Governors Association Center for Best Practices and Council of Chief State School Officers. Retrieved March 5, 2013 from www.corestandards.org/assets/CCSSI_ELA%20Standards.pdf

Fontichiaro, A. (2010). *Go straight to the source.* Ann Arbor, MI: Cherry Lake Publishing.

Gallagher, K. (2009). *Readicide: How schools are killing reading and what you can do about it.* Portland, ME: Stenhouse Publishers.

Robb, L. (2003). *Teaching reading in social studies, science, and math: Practical ways to weave comprehension strategies into your content area teaching.* New York: Scholastic.

Schmoker, M. (2011). *Focus: Elevating the essentials to radically improve student learning.* Alexandria, VA: Association of Supervision and Curriculum Development.

Tomlinson, C. A. (August, 2000). *Differentiation of instruction in the elementary grades.* ERIC Digest EDO-PS-00-7.

CHAPTER

Using the Text

Introduction: Because I Said So!

I have many interesting, thoughtful, engaging conversations with my students. However, I also have many conversations that go something like this: I ask a question, student gives correct answer, I ask why, student answers with "Because," I ask "Because why?" and student ends with "I don't know." Does this sound at all familiar? I thought so. Here's another outcome: suppose a student were to say to you instead, "I'm not sure. May I look in my book?" Would you say, "Go ahead"? I'll admit that, in the past, I would probably have been frazzled, and by no means would I have let the student look back in the book. If we've already covered something, the student should just know it, right?

For me, looking back in the book was as good as cheating. Now, I understand that looking back in the book can be a way of learning information. OK, so maybe they didn't learn it when they were supposed to, or maybe they memorized the information and have already forgotten it. This is another opportunity for students to make meaning with a text. Why not let them try again? Students are experts at memorizing answers and formulas for tests and then leaving the loads of information behind. However, if we encourage them to refer back to a text for information, we are not giving them the answer; they are finding it and in that process making a deeper connection with both the text and the content. We need to teach our students to make the connections that will enable them to make real meaning of the material. When students can't defend their answers or provide rationales for their ideas and opinions, they have not made meaning. Memorization has won the battle!

As teachers, we're not exactly innocent in the because-I-said-so department either. Think of my earlier story about rationalizing teaching certain materials and content in order to pass a standardized test. If students ask me why we're doing something, I should have a real-world reason for them to believe that the material I'm teaching is significant. "Because I said so" just isn't good enough. We need our students to understand why they're learning something, how to apply it to the real world and what they're going to be asked to do with their newfound knowledge. However, I admit that after being asked by a 2-year-old "why" 500 times, desperate times call for desperate measures, and "Because I said so" is inevitable.

This chapter will discuss ways to get away from "because I said so" and make real meaning with content and text. This chapter will begin with looking at exactly what teachers and students view as a text and why. Once we discuss what should and should not be considered a text, we can discuss the importance of why students need to be thinking about whether it is a primary or secondary source. We will discuss the importance of understanding author's purpose and intended audience and how to use each in your classroom. Finally, we will look at ways to get students referring back to and using their text for close readings, support, argumentation and research.

What Is a Text Anyway?

What's the first thing you think of when you hear the word "text"? It sounds so formal to me, my visualization goes right to a formal or "learning" body of writing—perhaps something I was assigned to read in college or a fancy, classical literary piece. Certainly "text" doesn't make me think of my beach book or the Sunday comics. My students, on the other hand, would go right to their cell phones.

Definitions offered by *Merriam-Webster* include the following:

> text *noun* \'tekst\ . . .
> **1 a** (1) **:** the original words and form of a written or printed work *(2)* **:** an edited or emended copy of an original work **b** **:** a work containing such text
> **2 a :** the main body of printed or written matter on a page **b :** the principal part of a book exclusive of front and back matter **c :** the printed score of a musical composition
> **3 a** (1) **:** a verse or passage of Scripture chosen especially for the subject of a sermon or for authoritative support (as for a doctrine) *(2)* **:** a passage from an authoritative source providing an introduction or basis (as for a speech) **b** **:** a source of information or authority
> **4:** THEME, TOPIC

5 a : the words of something (as a poem) set to music
b : matter chiefly in the form of words or symbols that is treated as data for processing by computerized equipment <*text*-editing software>
6 : a type suitable for printing running text
7 : textbook
8 a : something (as a story or movie) considered as an object to be examined, explicated, or deconstructed **b :** something likened to a text <the surfaces of daily life are *texts* to be explicated—Michiko Kakutani>
9 : FRAME OF REFERENCE 2 <updated to fit the women's lib *text* for consciousness raising—Judith Crist>

So a text can be quite complicated, or it can be viewed as pretty much anything with written words. However, the English Language Arts Common Core Standards for History/Social Studies and Science and Technical Subjects will have our students reading far more than just text. They can read movies, sculptures, paintings and other artwork, along with graffiti and soundtracks. Once students truly understand how to use and read a "text," they can analyze a number of different materials. For example, Fontichiaro (2010) says, "Paintings can be considered primary sources. Studying paintings and the people who created them can teach us a lot. We can learn about changing styles, themes, and ways of thinking" (p. 15).

When we're exposing our students to resources, we need to make it clear that each has its own purpose and message. When we ask students to go back and cite the text, they should understand that this does not necessarily have to be their textbook. A text could be a journal, comic, invitation or e-mail. Common texts in the content area classroom include textbooks, scholarly articles, newspaper articles, timelines, reference books, documentaries, historical documents and labeled diagrams. When you're trying to incorporate diverse materials into your teaching, consider pulling in texts that are not commonly found in the content area classroom. Some of those texts are listed in Table 5.1.

All of these ideas will get students comfortable with using and applying information from a variety of texts. Once they are comfortable, through modeling and practice, students will be able to easily refer back to the text as evidence. If students are exposed to a wide variety of materials and have a large selection of text available, they will be much more likely to refer back to it for evidence, defense and enhanced understanding.

TABLE 5.1 Content Texts

Nontypical Classroom Texts for Content Area Classrooms	Possible Application to Learning Academic Content
Novels	• Novels can be an excellent learning text in History classes and will give students a deeper understanding of the time period and events. Historical fiction can help reluctant students focus on events and make connections instead of trying to memorize information. • In the Science or Technical classroom, novels can supplement challenging material by making it more realistic. Consider reading a science fiction novel related to space or robotics with what you're covering or a survival novel when teaching about the earth. Students could keep a journal and compare texts.
Cartoons	• History teachers can use political cartoons for an introduction to units dealing with legislation or politics. They can also create cartoons based on what they're learning. • Science teachers may look at the science behind some of the funny cartoons with which students are familiar. Think: what would Charlie Brown have to do to kick the football before Lucy pulled it away? How fast would he have to be running?
Poetry	• Many historical accounts run through poetry that is available to History teachers, such as "Paul Revere's Ride" by Henry Wadsworth Longfellow. The poem presents the information quite differently than a textbook would and makes a great comparison and analysis piece. • Science and poetry have been friends since the beginning of time. Why do we insist on breaking them apart? How many poems can you find about the earth, stars, moon, ocean, rock and other elements? What is their connection to hard-core scientific facts?
Short stories	• Don't have time to spend reading an entire novel? I understand. So try a short story. If you find that it helps your students make connections and deepens student understanding, try a novel next time! Baby steps!
Diaries, journals and letters	• In a Social Studies or History classroom, diaries and journals give students an insight into how decisions were made and show the personal side of people who may not seem "real." • In a Science classroom, journals and letter correspondence may show students how a discovery was made, a hypothesis proved or research conducted. Understanding the scientist's thought process will likely help the students understand the science.

Nontypical Classroom Texts for Content Area Classrooms	Possible Application to Learning Academic Content
Recipes	• You may not have access to a kitchen in your classroom, but recipes can be wonderful enrichment in both the History and Science classrooms. In History, students may make a food item from a popular recipe of the time period or culture and bring it in to share with their peers. They may discuss how food and life would be different with only a wood-burning stove and having to use only natural resources. • Students in a Science classroom may use a recipe to create dough, chalk, paint, slime, mud or rock.
Directions	• Students are constantly asked to read and follow directions, but are they ever asked to analyze them for learning? In a History classroom, maybe you want to look at what Christopher Columbus told his men to do? Or the directions given when signing the Declaration of Independence? Or the directions ordered before going into a specific battle? • In a Science classroom, directions may be analyzed as to how the results would differ if even one tiny step was changed, and follow up with a discussion on how. Or perhaps you want to do research on how many discoveries were made because someone did *not* follow directions?
Advertisements	• Propaganda goes pretty closely with most History curriculum, and the comparisons to today's media are a great starting point for analysis. • How many advertisements do you see every day that support a specific scientific claim in order to sell you something? Would it be possible to find science to debunk the claim? Advertisements can be a great starting point for research and experimentation.
Brochures	• In many classes, students are asked to create brochures as part of research projects without ever having the opportunity to read them. In the era of technology, brochures are becoming less and less common. However, that doesn't mean that our students shouldn't be exposed to them as a learning tool for information. In History classes, reading brochures from the past will help students make connections and learn about the lifestyle of a given era. Students can also use brochures of historical landmarks and discuss places they would possibly like to visit or explore. • Science brochures are available with topics ranging from disease, volcanoes, rock climbing to genetically modified foods. Students can analyze how information is presented in brochures versus other texts.

Although they may not officially be considered text, students can read things like pieces of art, movies and cartoons. Remember that reading for learning, whether it is a formal text, picture or artifact, should be presented as an analytical task. Presenting these things as materials for reading will help students understand how to break down the work for closer analysis and comparison. When we talk about the traits of reading and what makes a good reader, the same skills apply to the analysis of a piece of art or film.

Primary and Secondary Sources

There are many different types of texts, and each can fit into one of two neat categories of primary or secondary sources. Although only the English Language Arts History/Social Studies Common Core Standards specifically state both types of sources, they should be used in all content area classrooms to broaden students' content reading. It is important for students to be able to distinguish primary from secondary sources. By understanding whether the text was created by someone firsthand, by an expert or by an outsider will help students make connections, recognize the author's purpose and intended audience and understand the content of the reading. Students should begin by asking themselves these questions as a starting point to decide whether a source is primary or secondary:

- Who wrote or created this material?
- In what time period was this material created?
- What type of material am I reading (journal, art, textbook, etc.)?

Fontichiaro (2010) defines primary sources as "original documents, objects, and other items that were created at the time being studied and that come directly from witnesses to the event or historical period" (p. 30). Primary sources include images, photographs, journals, diaries, original documents and interviews. There are many benefits to incorporating primary sources into your classroom. Primary sources give a firsthand account that many students can more easily connect with or relate to on a personal level. They may also make the content seem more realistic or significant to learning. According to Schmoker (2011), "About once a week, at most grade levels, students should have the chance to read from eyewitness or contemporary accounts, or from official or notable documents from historical periods they are studying" (p. 154). Primary sources are excellent texts for analysis and debate because often the author is not an expert but a witness, unlike secondary sources.

Fontichiaro (2010) goes on to define secondary sources as "an account or record of the past that was created after an event or historical period" (p. 30). Secondary sources include textbooks, encyclopedias, magazine articles and books. The majority of texts used in most classrooms would fall under the secondary source category. A great benefit of using secondary sources is that they are often written by an expert on the content. As Schmoker (2011) states, "Textbooks, along with other carefully selected nonfiction documents, afford students the kind of content-rich, semantically rich prose that students need to both acquire and critically process essential knowledge" (p. 129). Also, many secondary sources, like textbooks, often include examples of primary sources. For students to get a well-rounded view of the content, they should be exposed to a mixture of both primary and secondary sources. As discussed, unfortunately our students are not reading the primary sources included in their textbooks.

Analyzing and using primary and secondary sources will help students understand each individual text's validity. Determining whether a text is a primary or secondary source should impact the way the student reads it. When using a primary source, they may consider whether the author is biased, whether opinions are included or whether the author is a credible source. When using a secondary source, students may ask the same questions but may reasonably assume that they are dealing with more of an expert on the subject.

Author's Purpose and Intended Audience

You may have made the assumption that the terms "author's purpose" and "intended audience" belong in the English classroom and are not meant for content area teachers. I would agree that it may not be your responsibility to teach them, but I would highly encourage you to use them and discuss them frequently in your classroom. I would further assume that not all of your students have mastered an understanding of the concept of author's purpose or intended audience. Not only do these concepts help students comprehend a text; they also help the students see the significance in a piece of writing and question the author at a higher level of thinking.

Author's purpose is the reason an author decides to write, and it can be broken down into three large categories: to inform, to entertain, to persuade. When you are dealing with author's purpose, you can make answers as broad or as specific as you see fit for the content. Our students realize that we want them to learn from the materials we're working with each day, but do they ever think about why someone else wrote them or for whom they are intended? (The exception is our textbook, which was clearly written with the purpose of making their lives miserable!)

Every year when introducing author's purpose, I pass out a small piece of candy to each student, something small and plain like Hershey's Kisses, a piece of candy corn or a Skittle. Before the students eat them, I give each student a note card with one of the three types of author's purpose on it and ask them to free-write for 10 minutes about the candy using their assigned author's purpose. When they begin to moan and tell me how difficult the assignment is, I model an example of each purpose using the topic of a plain #2 pencil. My first story is about a lonely pencil that was left stranded on the floor of the locker room for several weeks, only to be found by a handsome, young man who, sadly, uses the pencil in a tragic pencil fight. The students quickly guess that my purpose was to be entertaining, although some strongly encourage me not to tell any more stories. (Trust me, a one-sentence summary really doesn't develop my highly entertaining narrative.) I then ask the students to guess my purpose for writing an informative essay about how pencils are made and a persuasive essay about how mechanical pencils are a waste of money. After the students have finished critiquing my writing, we brainstorm all the reasons, by category, that someone would write about a pencil. It is amazing how many reasons they come up with for each category! Once they're excited, I give them some time to write their own essays about the candy. The following day, we write again using a different purpose and share in small groups.

Although I use this activity in an ELA classroom, it could easily be applied to any content area. Consider how writing about the American Revolution using all three author's purposes would strengthen students' understanding of the material. For a persuasive piece, students would need to consider the people on each side of the war and why they were committed to their respective causes. What did the opposing side want? For what reasons should either be supported? An informative essay would give students the opportunity to clearly summarize the events of the American Revolution and prove comprehension. Content area classrooms are a great place for students to write with the purpose of entertaining because it is another great way to prove comprehension of the content. How can students write a story on a pioneer's life if they don't understand how a pioneer lived?

A science classroom could use the same activity on almost any subject, probably closer to the end of a unit, when students have attained a good understanding of the material. For example, students in a science classroom could write with different purposes on the topic of the changing of the earth's surface. For a persuasive piece, students could convince readers that we need to find a way to intervene in plate motions or to stop drilling in a specific area because of the effects on the earth's surface. A student would have to understand the content to persuade their reader either way. Writing an informative text would allow the students to summarize the information and could be presented in many different ways, including a formal essay, presentation, flowchart or digital map. You may not think that you have time for creative/entertaining writing, but not only does it help keep students engaged in what they're learning, it helps them understand and analyze materials. An entertaining piece on the earth's surface may be a firsthand account, as told by a volcano or rock surface, of how the weather, plate shifting and other geological events have changed them or made their life difficult or exciting. What have they lived through or seen in their lifetime? Once again, students would have to demonstrate an understanding of plate tectonics and more to make the story entertaining.

When looking at author's purpose, it is a good idea to have students actually write with a purpose to give them an idea of what an author is thinking when writing, whether it is the result of a lab or experiment or a letter to Congress. When students are asked to use a text for information, research or projects, understanding the author's purpose is crucial to how they read the information. Students need to be able to distinguish fact from opinion and make their own selections when completing research and labs. Understanding why an author is writing will enable students to make better decisions about how to use a text.

We can't talk about author's purpose without considering the intended audience—for whom is the author writing? Considering who the intended audience is for a piece of writing can, again, greatly help students comprehend a text. Was the author writing only for him- or herself, without intending that anyone else would see the work? Was the author writing for colleagues? Hoping to gain fame or fortune? Presenting to a group of elementary students? Writing to a worldwide audience with many different cultures and languages?

It could be difficult for students to use a text if they cannot first identify for whom the text is intended. Students analyzing a scientists' research notes may find them hard to decipher or confusing if they have been written in shorthand or using symbols. If they realize that the scientists' notes were meant for their own research, the fact that they created their own symbols would make much more sense. If students are reading an article from a scholarly journal containing vocabulary that is not familiar to them, they will understand why it is necessary to use context clues or a dictionary. Students should be reading and exploring texts in an analytical manner that encourages them to stop and ask questions, such as, "Why did the author do this? What can I take away from this material? Should I consider this a valid source?"

Understanding author's purpose and intended audience helps our students comprehend the texts they are reading. It also helps students to use and apply the texts in different situations depending on their own purpose for citing a text. I'm not saying that you have to spend time deciphering why textbooks are used in schools, but when it comes to primary sources in particular, spend some time analyzing the author's ideas and intentions. Baby steps will lead your students from trying to memorize words and ideas to trying to understand and analyze a text's content and purpose.

Text for Learning: Use It or Lose It

People say that with math, you either use it or lose it. Well, that's true about most things we learn. I've also heard that you never forget how to ride a bike; well, if you believe that, you should have seen me jump on a mountain bike after 15 years without riding. I'm confident that you would have been embarrassed for me. Learning from a text is the same thing; we have to constantly go back and apply what we've read, or it's like starting over. Every year we review parts of speech, and every year a few students can't identify words like prepositions or adverbs. I used to become frustrated, but then I had a student tell me, "Well, I haven't had to identify a preposition in like five years!" Even though I expect my students to be able to easily identify parts of speech, when they don't use it, it's easy to forget. Using a text or a variety of texts enables students to apply a variety of skills, such as justifying opinions, comparing points of view, note taking and finding information. We are going to discuss using the text with four categories: text for learning/close reading, text for support, text for argumentation, text for research.

Text for Close Reading

Using a text for close reading deepens students' comprehension of the content. You may want students to use their text for close reading when they are looking for information, preparing to cite information or determining meaning of the content. Students should use the before-, during- and after-reading strategies when doing a close reading, but there are a couple of other things to consider to help make the information clear. Thanks to the work of Kelly Gallagher (my hero), my students know that the first thing they should do when given a text is to number the paragraphs. This will make it easy to refer back to the text and find information. When students are reading, they should highlight what they believe is important. When you first begin this process, I recommend limiting how much students can highlight. I usually tell them only two or three sentences can be highlighted for every two or three paragraphs. If not, you will end up with 99% of the text highlighted. It takes experience for students to master picking out what is important when working with challenging texts. Students should annotate the text with comments, questions and main ideas as they are reading and jot down notes in the margins. If you are working with a text that students cannot write directly on, like a textbook, I recommend splurging for sticky notes. Students like using them—which, let's face it, helps the cause—and they will be reading and writing with the purpose of deciding what is most important.

The worksheet in Figure 5.1 is an example of something History students could complete after or during a close reading of the Declaration of Independence (Appendix A9, p. 141). I used the text in correlation with *Chains* by Laurie Halse Anderson (2008).

Using the text for close reading helps our students deepen comprehension and apply their knowledge by easily referring back to the text. The activity in Figure 5.1 could fit into more than one of our using-the-text categories, but in order to really comprehend the material, a close reading is needed. It forces students to continually go back to the document, looking at specific sections, headings and vocabulary to defend their own opinions, simultaneously deepening their understanding of the content.

You can use almost any text for a close reading, but the text should not be too long. For middle and high school students, I would not recommend more than two to four pages. In a science classroom, consider the benefits of completing a close reading of student lab results. Students could be asked to highlight what they believe to be the most important steps, comment and question what went wrong or right, determine what could be done differently and analyze the outcome, all strengthening their grasp of the experiment or lab. I recommend trying close readings with different levels of text complexity and using the students' responses to help guide you in your further reading selections. Using a wide variety of texts for close readings will improve academic content comprehension.

The Declaration of Independence

Objectives: Students will demonstrate the ability to . . .

Compare and contrast text features, including format and headers in terms of their structure and purpose.

Identify organizational structure and evaluate its effectiveness.

Compare and contrast the treatment, scope and organization of ideas from different sources on the same topic.

Assess the adequacy and appropriateness of an author's details.

Identify the author's purpose and intended audience for the text.

Analyze the author's argument, perspective or viewpoint and explain the development of key points.

Recognize how writers cite facts and present opinions in informational text.

Use the Declaration of Independence to answer the questions below:

1. List the four headings from the Declaration of Independence. Then, state the purpose of each heading. Explain why you think this heading is appropriate.

Heading	Purpose	Is Heading Appropriate?	Support Your Answer.

2. Assess the organizational structure of the Declaration of Independence.

3. Describe how the patriots and loyalists are portrayed in *Chains*. Compare that to how they are each portrayed in the Declaration of Independence. (Think, good guys, bad guys)

	Chains	Declaration of Independence
Patriots		

FIGURE 5.1 Sample Activity

| Loyalists | | |

4. Who is the intended audience of the Declaration of Independence, the whole world, the king, the British, the Americans? Cite two examples directly from the text that justify your answer.

5. Identify and describe the purpose of the Declaration of Independence. In your opinion, was the purpose met? Cite at least three details from at least two different sources to support your answer.

6. How do the details within the List of Grievances adequately support the resolution posed by the Patriots? Defend your answer with details from the text.

7. Cite four words, phrases or sentences that show the authors opinions.

> Ex. "the merciless, Indian savages" – the author obviously does not think highly of Native Americans. I can infer this because of the words, "merciless" and "savage."
>
> 1.
> 2.
> 3.
> 4.

FIGURE 5.1 (Continued)

Text for Support

By completing close readings, students will be able to easily use the text to support their own answers and opinions. Using the text for support will likely be applied once students have finished a reading but will encourage them to refer back to their text to defend or explain their conclusions. Often, text for support is used in question-and-answer type situations. Remember, with the English Language Arts Common Core Standards for History/Social Studies and Science and Technical Subjects, students will be using their texts *constantly*. The text is a crucial component to learning and applying content knowledge.

Students may walk away from a text with a general idea, theme or analysis, but when asked to use the document to support their answers, they're really asking themselves, "Why do I think this?" They are making a connection to the text, their knowledge and their own opinions. Using the text for support would include activities and questions that ask the student to justify or defend an answer or opinion, analyze what led them to a specific conclusion or make connections from the text to the real world. In reaching a general idea about a topic, students should be able to explain how they reached their conclusion with examples from the text.

Text for Argumentation

Although students use the text to support their arguments, I like to consider text for argumentation a separate category. Using the text for argumentative purposes is unique because students get to present the information with their own spin or purpose. When using the text for argumentative purposes, students must decide what information is best suited to strengthen their case or show weakness in an opposing view. Students have to consider the components that will make their argument stronger and research numerous texts to see which is the most useful. Using the text for argumentation includes working on debates, argumentative or persuasive writing and critiquing the author or a scientific process.

When using the text for support or argumentation, students are often looking for a specific detail to make their case stronger. Often, using the text for argumentative purposes is part of a research process. Both primary and secondary sources can be used for argumentation. Considering the type of text helps students analyze how best to use the source in their argument.

Text for Research

Using a text for research is a matter of using the text to find, gather and learn information on a given topic. When using a text for research, students have to analyze the usefulness, validity and accuracy of the text. Other skills include History/Social Studies and Science and Technical Standard 8: Distinguish among facts, reasoned judgments based on research, opinion and speculation in a text. Again, both primary and secondary sources can be used for research.

Examples of using a text for research purposes are research papers, document analysis, flowcharts and projects. Using the text for research is another great way for students to see the value in a wide variety of texts and examine the usefulness of each through exploration.

Activities to Teach Students to Cite the Text

In connection with encouraging our students to continually use the text, we need to make sure we're teaching them how to cite and incorporate the text into their daily work. One of the easiest and most efficient ways to begin this process is to provide students with sentence stems that they can use in their writing or in class discussions. I like to start by giving my students a certain number of stems that are required in various assignments, and, as time goes by, citing the text becomes natural. Sentence stems include:

- According to the author, . . .
- On page xx, paragraph xx states . . .
- The article/book/text said . . .
- From the reading, I know . . .
- The author said . . .

This may sound like an elementary beginning to some of you, but remember that, since kindergarten, most of our students have not been taught to refer back to the text. To many, this will be somewhat of a new tool. We are taking baby steps to get our students to use the text; it is up to you where to begin the process of citing the text. If you are working on a more formal piece of writing, research or project, have your students work on their citations as they work on the research, writing or any other activity they are completing. Too often, students are taught to cite the text at the end of their learning or project. By the time students go back to interact with the text, the connection has been lost, and the material cannot be easily sorted. Graphic organizers or online programs work best to keep sources straight when working with multiple texts. A helpful online citation and research website is www.zotero.org. If your students are organizing their information and sources by hand, provide them with a graphic organizer for notes and citations. A sample graphic organizer is shown in Figure 5.2 and can also be found in Appendix A10 (p. 143). Students should use a different graphic organizer for each text.

This graphic organizer should be passed out before students begin using the text. If you are using texts with more than one class that cannot leave the room, this will be especially helpful for students to return to working with their information.

Other activities that encourage students to cite the text are note taking, debate and author battles. Author battles are when students are given at least two different texts with some opposing views or evidence. Then they are asked to pick a side and discuss it in a large or small group. The students are forced to refer back to their texts for their pros and cons. There are many ways to get your students citing and referring back to a text.

Topic _____

Source

[   ]

I selected this source because

_____
_____

Central Ideas/Summary of Text

_____
_____
_____
_____
_____

Direct Quote and Page #	Direct Quote and Page #	Direct Quote and Page #

FIGURE 5.2 Citation Graphic Organizer

The first step—baby steps, remember—is to get your students using a wide variety of sources. It's up to you whether you want to jump right in with everything at once or ease your way in to using and citing multiple texts.

Review: What to Do, What to Do!

- Broaden your view of text. Try incorporating new texts into your curriculum.
- Make sure your that students understand the differences between primary and secondary sources and that they have the opportunity to work with both frequently.
- Encourage your students to make connections with the writer and text by analyzing author's purpose and intended audience, deepening their understanding of the text.
- Use each text with purpose: text for close reading, text for support, text for argumentation and text for research.

References

Anderson, L. A. (2008). *Chains.* New York: Simon & Schuster.

Common Core State Standards Initiative. (2010). *Common core state standards for English language arts literacy in history/social studies, science, and technical subjects.* Washington, DC: National Governors Association Center for Best Practices and Council of Chief State School Officers. Retrieved March 5, 2013 from www.corestandards.org/assets/CCSSI_ELA%20Standards.pdf

Fontichiaro, A. (2010). *Go straight to the source.* Ann Arbor, MI: Cherry Lake Publishing.

Merriam-Webster.com. (2013). Retrieved July 8, 2013 from www.merriam-webster.com/dictionary/text

Schmoker, M. (2011). *Focus: Elevating the essentials to radically improve student learning.* Alexandria, VA: Association of Supervision and Curriculum Development.

CHAPTER 6

All A's! Absorb, Analyze, Argue and Apply!

Introduction: All A's, a Four-Step Process

All A's. It sounds good, right? Teachers love when students earn A's, but these A's are meant for teachers. This chapter will focus on how teachers can use a concept of All A's to get students using higher-level thinking skills in a multistep process. All A's is a process for teachers to use when planning a learning activity or unit and a process for students to use when taking in and demonstrating new knowledge.

The first step in All A's is for students to spend time absorbing information. That is followed by analysis, whose goal is to get students analyzing information in ways to form opinions and hypotheses. The last two components of All A's are the argue and apply pieces. Arguing and applying the content will allow students to demonstrate their knowledge in diverse ways and use higher-level thinking skills to make connections to what they've learned. I would not expect you to use this strategy with every small concept you teach but to take it into consideration when planning units or assessing big ideas. It is by no means a fix-all. However, I truly believe that if you take these steps into consideration when planning and teaching, your students will be more prepared to master the English Language Arts Common Core Standards for History/Social Studies and Science and Technical Subjects. Appendixes A11–A16 (pp. 144–154) contain blank All A's charts for the History/Social Studies and Science and Technical areas at several grade levels.

Step 1: Absorb

We all teach differently. Some of us may have more in common than others, but when it comes down to it, we all have our own spin on how to do things. That's one of the greatest things about being a teacher! Personally, I spend a lot of time in absorption mode. I want to make sure things sink in and my students really get it. The problem is that sometimes we never move past absorption mode and allow our students to work with the knowledge that they've gained. The Common Core Standards do not encourage absorbing information, testing and moving on. Students need to spend time working, creating and applying with what they've learned. Some students don't fully "get it" until they're given the chance to move on to the analysis step.

With absorption, students are metaphorical sponges, soaking up knowledge. To absorb information, students need basic exposure, readings and experience. Students can absorb information in a variety of ways, including reading, hearing, viewing, summarizing and discussing. The key to absorbing information is that our students are not passively taking notes or reading without purpose; to fully absorb new content, students need to be making meaning with what they're learning. I would encourage you to use many of the prereading and during-reading activities discussed in Chapter 3 to help students absorb the information they are reading.

Often, hearing information is not enough to build content comprehension in many of our students. However, if students are engaged in what they're listening to, whether an audio recording, story or lecture, they are much more likely to absorb information. Perhaps as in introduction to a Civil Rights unit, you play an audio recording of Martin Luther King's "I Have a Dream" speech. As you play the audio, stop and discuss the big ideas and themes of the speech with your students to ensure that they are absorbing the information and content. By hearing the speech instead of reading or discussing it, students will make connections to when the audience cheers and to the power and tone of the speaker's voice. Remember that absorbing is the first step in a process and that we cannot yet expect our students to be masters of the content. Baby steps. Exposing students to information in any fashion is not enough for most to achieve mastery.

Absorption can also take place through viewing information or content. Students are often shown video clips or pictures at the beginning of a unit to spark ideas or interest, and it is indeed a form of absorbing information. It is crucial when using viewing as a tool for absorbing information that students understand the purpose of viewing the material to be shown. I understand that we like our students to be hands-on learners and that they often learn through doing, but consider switching things up and using different tools for different materials. In a science classroom, consider showing your students a lab or experiment by allowing them to watch while you complete the experiment yourself. There are many pros to students' viewing a lab instead of completing it. No one student dominates and does all of the work. All the students have the chance to learn and take in the information in a way they can personally connect with, and students can interpret the results of a lab without others' bias.

Summarizing is a good way for students to absorb information because they really have to think about what's been presented, whether it is from reading, hearing or viewing. Absorbing information through summarizing can be completed through writing, brainstorming, journaling, discussing or note taking.

The last form of absorption takes place through discussion. In many classes, discussions are the ending point of learning material, but I would encourage you to begin a discussion at the start of your unit and go back to it continually. Discussing new content gives students the opportunity to hear, talk and think about material in their heads and voice their own opinions when they feel ready. If they don't "get it" at the beginning, by hearing their peers thoughts, they may be able to make a connection that they couldn't in any other way.

Students can absorb information in many ways, but most would fit into one of these categories. Students should be exposed to many different tools in the absorption period to ensure that every one of them has absorbed as much about the content as they can before moving on to analyzing the information.

Step 2: Analyze

The goal of the analysis stage is for students to take the knowledge they've absorbed in the first step and use it to form opinions, hypotheses and critiques. Johnson (2013) maintains that "analytical thinkers are investigators, organizers, categorizers, labelers, and specifiers, but they only do these things within what they have experienced" (p. 6). Basically, once the students have taken in or absorbed the information, they need the chance to engage with the content. Key strategies to analyze information are questioning, inferring, connecting, assessing and comparing and contrasting. Students can use these strategies in a variety of ways, including graphic organizers, discussions, research, essays, labs, projects and many others.

When students are asked to analyze information or content knowledge, they are breaking the information down into parts and understanding how the concept works together as a whole, leading to a deeper understanding of the content. Questioning content information helps students learn to think on their own. The English Language Arts Common Core Standards for History/Social Studies and Science and Technical Subjects ask that students be independent thinkers and that they are able to develop and defend ideas of their own. Johnson (2013) states that "the role of teacher is to show students analytical thinking strategies and techniques and then create learning opportunities that require students to use them in order to learn content and gain abilities" (p. 8).

Teaching students to question content is the first step toward independent thinking. Too many students have learned to get by in school by simply memorizing the material and never questioning teacher or text. I'll admit that, at times, I have become upset with students for constantly asking questions or not letting me finish a lesson because they have a question or comment. It has taken time and practice to encourage this type of whole-class learning and questioning skills that allow us to have a type of productive whole-group learning and teaching. Our students should be encouraged to take the risk of asking questions; as you know, that in itself can be frightening for many students. To give students the confidence to question content—whether it is something they don't understand, something they are looking for a reason for or a relationship with something they wonder about or find interesting—it should be understood that there are no dumb questions. However, to ensure that questions are thought provoking, students should be taught to ask themselves the following before asking their question to the teacher or class:

- Can this answer be found in the text itself?
- How is this question related to the content we're learning (connections)?

Having asked both questions, students should be able to determine whether it's appropriate for the teacher and class or they can answer it themselves. Students can apply questioning skills by writing questions to the author or scientist, questioning while reading, questions for someone who lived during the time period or questioning the validity of information, just to name a few suggestions.

Once students have developed their questioning skills, take them a bit further (baby steps) to inferring. Making inferences requires students to use evidence and reasoning to draw a conclusion. It is important that students understand that inferring and predicting are not the same. For students to make a valid, evidence-based inference, they must first analyze the information to make a decision or draw a conclusion.

Another way for students to analyze information is to make a connection to the content. They are basically breaking down the content to see in what ways it can relate to the real world or to their own personal experiences. This strategy also makes learning the material seem more significant because the student can make a personal relationship with the material. It may seem difficult for students to make a personal connection to something that at first they have little interest in and have no idea how it applies to them: the Battle of Gettysburg, volcanoes, electricity. Here's what's key: allow your students to make connections to *anything* and fit it into their learning process. The connection may at first not seem strong to you, but it's about what's significant to the learner. I've allowed my students to connect content to video games, television shows, movies, food, pieces of art, personal experiences, places and songs. You may be surprised at the amazing connections they make when given the chance to explain and how much more thoughtful their responses and analysis become when given the opportunity to build a relationship with the content. A sample graphic organizer for making connections is shown in Figure 6.1. This can also be found in Appendix A17 (p. 156). In completing the graphic organizer and making connections, students are analyzing information to strengthen their comprehension of the topic.

Another strategy for the analysis step of All A's is assessing the material and content being taught. As I'm sure you know, students love to be the ones determining the value of their learning and materials. Through assessing a text or content, students are analyzing the validity, accuracy and quality of the text or material. Allowing students to assess materials or content can be scary for some teachers and understandably so; it takes time for students to understand how to assess fairly and accurately and can be quite a tiresome process. Let's face it: kids can be ruthless at times. It is important for your students to understand that, when you ask them to assess something, you're not asking whether they liked it or not but rather about quality. This is a task that requires modeling and patience; don't expect your students to be experts on the first try. In my own experience, students can be quite critical. Students could be asked to assess the procedures a scientist took to complete a lab, the way an author presented material, how a president handled a crisis or any variety of text.

The final strategy in the analyze step is comparing and contrasting. Students learn to compare and contrast at a very young age and understand it as a strategy for comprehending and analyzing information. Through compare-and-contrast activities, students are forced to look at the details of the content and relate them to other events, experiments or concepts. Working through comparison activities also helps students straighten out details that they may have found confusing by examining how they are alike or different from other things. Compare-and-contrast activities can

Topic: _____

Directions: In each column, make a connection from the text/content to the topic or item listed in the heading. Then, explain the relationship or connection and cite evidence in the text that led you to making the connection.

	Connection	Relationship	Text that led me to making this connection
TV Show			
Movie			
Place			
Song			
Different Content Area			
Video Game, Personal Experience or Free Choice			

FIGURE 6.1 Connections Graphic Organizer

be simple Venn diagrams, other graphic organizers or something as complex as a research essay or debate.

No matter what strategy you choose to use to get your students analyzing content—and I hope you choose to use many—students will walk away with a deeper understanding of the material. With analysis skills, students are breaking down and examining content to build relationships and comprehension. Once they really are building mastery of content, they are ready to argue and apply their knowledge.

Step 3: Argue

The third step in the All A's process is to argue. Most kids like to argue, right? If you work with teenagers or have any of your own, you know the answer. The ability to argue effectively, especially when focusing on content, is a skill for students who are ready to show mastery of what they've learned and implement that knowledge into a well formed thought backed by reason and evidence. Arguing teaches students to use numerous skills, including justification, organization and creation. Schmoker (2011) states that "students need plenty of opportunities to read and argue about what they find in a variety of source documents, past and present" (p. 152). It is our job to provide students with the opportunity and skills to effectively argue. Although students can form and develop arguments in many ways, in this section we are going to focus on argumentative writing and debate.

For students to be able to write an effective argument, they must first understand how to organize their information. It is not your responsibility as a content area teacher to spend a semester teaching argumentative writing, but if students can understand four basic components, they can write an effective argument. Students need to understand that an effective argument contains (1) an argumentative statement or claim, (2) reasons or reasoning, (3) facts to support each reason and (4) the addressing of counterclaims or counterarguments. When assigning argumentative writing, you have many choices. Students can write from their own perspective, be forced to play devil's advocate, or write as a person in the content area, such as a scientist or historical character. It is also up to you how detailed you would like to get in the assignment. Argumentative essays can be completed in one class period or take an entire week of drafting, editing, fact checking and so on. The outline in Figure 6.2 is a very basic template for setting up an argumentative piece of writing and can also be used for organizing information. This outline can also be found in Figure 6.2. This outline can be used in preparation for an argumentative essay, debate or even classroom discussion. It can also be modified to be as simple or complex as you'd like it.

Back to the baby steps.

Debate is a structured argument. Critical thinking is crucial when preparing for debate. One of the first things I like to do when introducing debate to my classroom is to watch some examples, both good and bad. You can find many high school debates online or, if you are up to it, watch a political debate. How much time you want to devote to debating is, again, up to you. You may want students to role-play during a quick 10-minute

Topic: _____

Argument or Claim:

Intended Audience:

Purpose:

Reason #1: _____

　　　Fact or Support: _____

　　　Citation: _____

| Counterargument | → | How I will address counterargument |

Reason #2: _____

　　　Fact or Support: _____

　　　Citation: _____

FIGURE 6.2 Argument Graphic Organizer

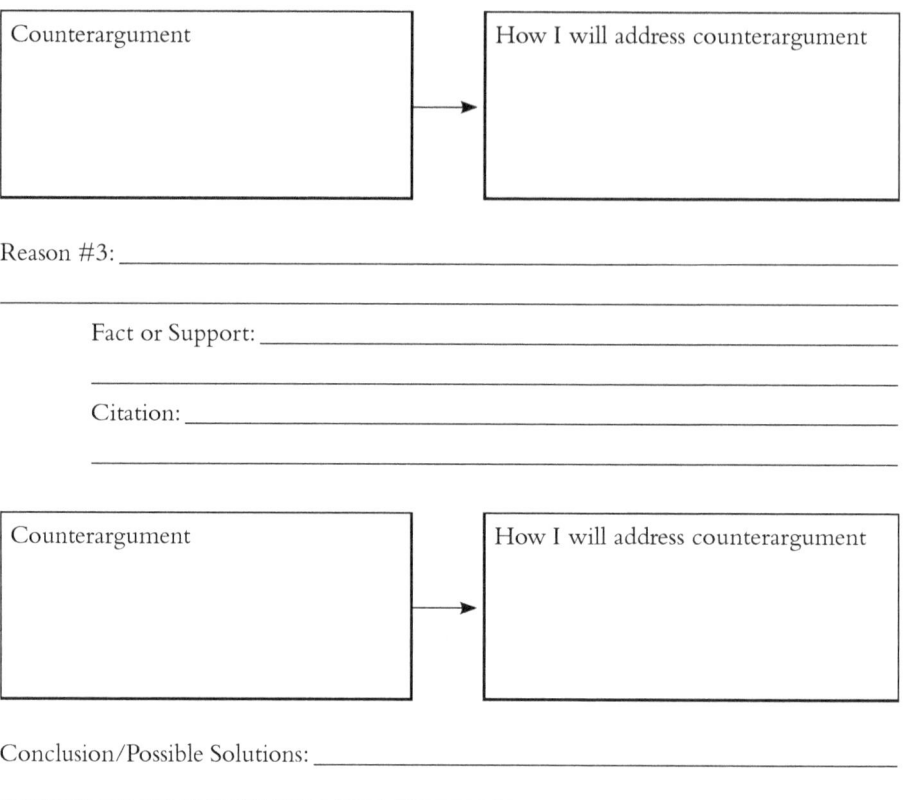

FIGURE 6.2 (Continued)

debate over the Civil War or spend weeks reviewing materials, organizing information and practicing for a 50-minute debate. You can choose to make your debates formal, with specific time limits and structure, or conduct debating strategies in small- or large-group discussions.

Regardless of how you structure argument and debate, students are working with the material they've learned and using their critical thinking skills. Argument can be powerful, whether it is in written or verbal form, and teaches students the skills they need to be college and career ready.

Step 4: Apply

The final step in All A's is to apply! I realize that according to Bloom's Taxonomy, application is right in the center of critical thinking skills. However, as we discuss application, we will be focusing on how students apply their learning of content to even bigger and more complex learning and structures. Students apply knowledge in a million different ways, but how often do they get to come up with their own inquiry-based learning projects or tools? Step 4 of All A's asks students to apply their content knowledge to make a decision about something related that they would like to further investigate. As a teacher, it can be a bit scary to give students this type of freedom, but the rewards for both teacher and student are worth it.

When you begin allowing your students to make their own decisions about learning, you will get some resistance. Even though our students complain—some more than others—they *want* us to tell them what to do and how to do it to earn their grades. Most students are not familiar with the idea that they can use their knowledge and apply it to something of their own interest. In this sense, the application step is not just "Pick anything you want in the world and learn about it." I encourage you to use inquiry-based learning and projects in such a way that content is still connected and structured. I also encourage you to approve all projects before students begin working and be lenient if a student begins and feels the need to switch topics. I like to let students work in groups or alone when completing projects, and I admit to being surprised by how many students choose to work alone or leave a group because they don't share the same interests. How rewarding when a student would rather learn something they're interested in than be in a group with their best friend. I consider that progress! It takes students some time to understand the freedom they are being given.

Before beginning, you will need to decide how structured you want your inquiry work to be, some teachers may be ready to really turn their students loose, while others (like me) would rather have more of a controlled environment. As mentioned, this inquiry focus will be limited to applying the content knowledge they have gained in steps 1–3 of All A's. For example, if you are completing a unit of study on the Great Depression, you may begin by asking your students to evaluate the content and discuss their thoughts and opinions about the unit. If you are feeling relaxed, you may want to let your students select any question they want connected to the Great Depression. Or if you'd like to take baby steps, perhaps begin by giving your students five or six options to choose from and allow them to think up other topics for approval by you. In studying the Great Depression, students may want to learn more about the stock market (Is the stock market still significant on a global level?), the war (How was the war related to the Great Depression?), the economy (What factors contribute to the ups and downs of the economy? How has the economy impacted people in my community?), economics (How do production and distribution impact me as a buyer?), bankruptcy (What is the process of borrowing money? Should people be allowed to file bankruptcy?), Franklin Roosevelt (Was Roosevelt responsible for the Depression?) or the effects on the rest of the world (How does one country's economy impact economies in the rest of the world?).

You will also have to determine your requirements for how students do their investigations and how the outcomes of their inquiries are demonstrated. Again, you don't have to give up all the power; you get to decide how much freedom your students can handle. Some classrooms thrive without limits, and others need to be reigned in. Neither is right or wrong but rather more a choice in teaching and learning styles. Regardless of what you choose, it is important that students know the procedures and expectations from the start.

Once students have picked their topic for inquiry, you must remember that it can lead them into a lot of different places, and you must be OK with that as long as they can tie everything back to the content. Remember, the connection to the content is important so that students can see the importance and connections in what they've learning and investigating.

It is also your responsibility to help students understand how they can gather information. Will they have access to the library, Internet, and reference materials? Can students complete fieldwork, interviews and labs to gather information? Will you be supplying them, or will they need their own sources? How should their sources be documented?

Finally, how will your students demonstrate what they've learned and connect it to the content? Will you give them choices or have strict requirements? Personally, I recommend assigning a required essay and then allowing students to pick one other form of demonstrating information. I think by having students provide an essay of what they've learned, they are able to present their ideas clearly, and often the process of writing helps students bring their ideas together and can aid them in their projects. When we're talking about demonstrating knowledge, I'd like to focus on the idea of creation and I don't mean "creating" a PowerPoint presentation. Students should not parrot information but actually show you what they've learned as a process from beginning to end. The goal is discovery. Students could be asked to demonstrate a lab; build a structure; create a blog, journal or video; navigate a website; or design a solution.

If you're hesitant to work with inquiry-based projects, I encourage you to find a science teacher! Some teachers associate inquiry-based projects with English and Social Studies, but science teachers are often the experts. Science fairs are a great example of inquiry projects at their finest. The key is collaboration! If you work in a team where a group of teachers share the same students, this is an even greater opportunity for collaboration in a multiclass inquiry-based project approach. In the apply step of All A's, students are using the information they've gained and demonstrating that it is applicable to them by making a connection with a real-world problem. If our ultimate goal is that students are college and career ready, connecting and applying knowledge through inquiry projects are crucial.

Back to Unit Planning

Let's go back once again to unit planning. The big picture is so important! You wouldn't plan a vacation without looking at a road map right? When planning a unit, teachers need to look at the big picture and consider how they want the lesson and the student's learning to progress. By determining what activities they will be completing and what strategies they will be using under each category of All A's, teachers will be able to organize learning as a process and ensure that students are using a variety of higher-level thinking skills to build on what they're learning. Table 6.1 presents a sample progression using All A's on a few of the Grades 6–8 History/Social Studies Common Core Standards. Table 6.2 presents the progression of All A's in some of the Common Core Standards for Science and Technical Subjects, Grades 9–10.

The concept of All A's can be used when planning any lesson or when working with any content. I recommend taking some time to explain the concept of All A's to the students in your classroom and to help them to understand how they fit with your goals of working toward inquiry. We know that learning is a process, but I hope that you can use All A's in your unit planning to make the process more understandable and defined.

TABLE 6.1 Grades 6–8 History/Social Studies

Grades 6–8	Absorb	Analyze	Argue	Apply
1. Cite specific textual evidence to support analysis of primary and secondary sources.	Teacher presents mini lesson over primary and secondary sources while students complete guided notes.	Students compare and contrast various sources and assess their validity and strength through analysis.	Students use and cite primary and secondary sources to argue a topic related to the academic content.	Students cite textual evidence from a variety of sources to solve a problem related to the academic content.
2. Determine the central ideas or conclusions of a text; provide an accurate summary of the text distinct from prior knowledge or opinions.	Students read a chapter from their history books on the Jamestown colony and write a summary of what they have read.	Students connect the events and people of the Jamestown colony to other events in history and discuss the outcomes.	Students write argumentative essays about whether the settlers should have left the colony to avoid famine, disease or war with the Native Americans or stayed to try to find a better life in America.	Students will complete an inquiry-based project on the questions, "Are people searching for the perfect life today? What sacrifices do settlers make for the good of their family?"
3. Identify key steps in a text's description of a process related to History/Social Studies.	Students watch a video explaining how a bill becomes a law.	Students complete a graphic organizer of the steps and then rank them from least to most important.	Students debate whether the process for how a bill becomes a law is fair, stating text-based evidence and steps of how a law is currently made.	Students complete an inquiry-based project to answer the question, based on a worldwide structure, "What is the best or fairest way to create a law?"
4. Determine the meaning of words and phrases as they are used in a text, including vocabulary specific to domains related to history/social studies.	Students use context clues during reading to figure out unknown words. They may check their answers in the glossary or a dictionary.	Students draw a picture to represent the word, act out the word, list synonyms and antonyms of the word and list topics that could be connected to the word or phrase.	Students write an argumentative essay where they are required to use at least 5–10 vocabulary words to demonstrate comprehension of their meaning.	Students complete an inquiry-based project to answer, "How do events, or how does history, change language?"

5. Describe how a text presents information (e.g., sequentially, comparatively, causally).	Ask students to put the information they are reading onto a graphic organizer as they read.	Discuss why each student selected the graphic organizer and analyze which were the most effective and why.	Give students a list of 5–10 topics. In small or large groups, allow students to argue the most logical way to present the information.	Investigate how intended meaning can be changed by changing the text structure of a given text. Complete interviews, surveys and discussions to analyze how text structure changes meaning.
6. Identify aspects of a text that reveal an author's point of view or purpose (e.g., loaded language, inclusion or avoidance of particular facts).	Assign students to read *Common Sense* by Thomas Payne.	Students will reread the text and highlight loaded language in pink, facts in yellow, and counterarguments in blue. In the left margin, students will write the purpose and in the right margin their own personal opinions of the text and its meaning.	In a class discussion, argue the effectiveness of Payne's writing. Analyze what specific content made it so popular.	Ask students to create an inquiry-based project that answers the question, "How do events or strategies sway people or bring them to action?"
7. Integrate visual information (e.g., in charts, graphs, photographs, videos, or maps) with other information in print and digital texts.	Expose students to a wide variety of visual information including charts, graphs, photographs, videos, maps and other digital media.	Assign students to make a print text more effective by creating a form of visual information and then justify what they created and how it contributes to overall comprehension of the content.	Show students multiple sources of visual information to accompany a print text. Allow students to argue which form of visual information is most effective, citing details from the texts.	Students create an inquiry-based project to answer the questions, "What makes information appealing? How do you sell information?"

(Continued)

TABLE 6.1 (Continued)

Grades 6–8	Absorb	Analyze	Argue	Apply
8. Distinguish among fact, opinion, and reasoned judgment in a text.	Students watch a political debate.	Teacher gives each student a transcript of the debate. Students will highlight facts in pink, opinions in yellow and reasoned judgments in blue.	Students will use the information gathered from the Apply activity to argue which candidate won the debate.	Students will create an inquiry-based project that answers the question, how do we form opinions?
9. Analyze the relationship between a primary and secondary source on the same topic.	Teacher presents a lesson on primary and secondary sources while students complete a Venn diagram of the information.	After reading a primary and secondary sources on the same topic, students create a three-column flow chart with details of each text and their connections.	Students debate the validity of several secondary and primary sources on the same topic.	Students complete an inquiry-based project that attempts to answer, "Does bias impact the way students learn content?"

TABLE 6.2 Grades 9–10 Science and Technical Subjects

Grades 9–10	Absorb	Analyze	Argue	Apply
1. Cite specific textual evidence to support analysis of science and technical texts, attending to the precise details of explanations or descriptions.	Teachers provide students with a list of evidence-based sentence stems like, "According to the author . . ."	Students complete the same experiment, with different directions and analyze the outcomes based on the preciseness of details, explanations and descriptions.	Students are provided several texts on the same topic to read. They argue which text gives the most precise details, explanations and descriptions.	Students complete an inquiry-based project attempting to answer, "How have accidents impacted science?"
2. Determine the central ideas or conclusions of a text; trace the text's explanation or depiction of a complex process, phenomenon, or concept; provide an accurate summary of the text.	Students read a text on climate change and write a summary of the reading, including how the text works through a complex process.	Students complete a flowchart of the information that demonstrates how it works through a specific process.	Students debate the validity of the process and how it is presented in the text.	Students complete an inquiry-based project in attempt to answer, "Is drawing conclusions scientific?"
3. Follow precisely a complex multistep procedure when carrying out experiments, taking measurements, or performing technical tasks, attending to special cases or exceptions defined in the text.	Students watch the teacher complete a multistep lab or experiment.	Students attempt to complete a multistep lab based only on a text, without speaking or asking for clarification. When finished, they will analyze how accurately they each completed the multistep procedure.	Students debate the best way to complete multistep procedures, considering written or verbal directions, graphics, measurements, visuals and vocabulary.	Students create labs or experiments with multistep procedures for their peers to complete and then analyze which directions worked most effectively and why.

(*Continued*)

TABLE 6.2 (Continued)

Grades 9–10	Absorb	Analyze	Argue	Apply
4. Determine the meaning of symbols, key terms, and other domain-specific words and phrases as they are used in a specific scientific or technical context relevant to *grades 9–10 texts and topics*.	Students will use context clues to infer the meaning of unknown words, phrases and symbols. When applicable, students will check their answers in a glossary or dictionary.	Students will connect symbols, vocabulary and phrases to a picture or synonym that helps them comprehend meaning.	Students will write an argumentative essay using 5–10 symbols, key terms or phrases.	Students complete an inquiry-based project attempting to answer, "Are symbols beneficial to science?"
5. Analyze the structure of the relationships among concepts in a text, including relationships among key terms (e.g., *force, friction, reaction force, energy*).	Annotate a text while reading.	Students create a flowchart of the information they've read showing the connections and relationships among concepts and key terms.	Students debate how concepts are connected in a class discussion while assessing each concept's importance to the whole.	Students attempt to complete an inquiry-based project on a specific content related question.
6. Analyze the author's purpose in providing an explanation, describing a procedure, or discussing an experiment in a text, defining the question the author seeks to address.	Read a text while making annotations.	Discuss the author's purpose in small groups after reading.	Debate whether the author met his or her purpose through the text, analyzing what he or she could have done to make the concept clearer.	Students complete an inquiry-based project attempting to answer how should scientific information be presented?
7. Assess the extent to which the reasoning and evidence in a text support the author's claim or a recommendation for solving a scientific or technical problem.	Students read a short text.	Students assess the value of the author's work by determining what letter grade they would earn for their work.	Students debate with their peers the grade the author should earn based on the author's reasoning and evidence to support the claim.	Students complete an inquiry-based project attempting to answer, "Why must science be solved?"

Review: What to Do, What to Do!

- All A's is a teaching and planning strategy that works as a progressive model for student learning.
- Step 1—Absorb: Provide students with numerous opportunities to soak in new information.
- Step 2—Analyze: Allow students to work with new information in several ways to develop opinions, hypotheses and connections.
- Step 3—Argue: Use argument for students to show mastery through well formed thought backed by reason and evidence. Arguing teaches students to use numerous skills including justification, organization and creation.
- Step 4—Apply: Ask that students apply their content knowledge to make a decision about something related to that knowledge that they would like to further investigate. Have students complete their own inquiry-based projects connected to content previously learned in class.
- When planning units, consider how you will take students through the process of All A's to build on their critical thinking in order to ultimately apply their knowledge to their own inquiry-based learning and connections.

References

Common Core State Standards Initiative. (2010). *Common core state standards for English language arts literacy in history/social studies, science, and technical subjects.* Washington, DC: National Governors Association Center for Best Practices and Council of Chief State School Officers. Retrieved March 5 2013, from www.corestandards.org/assets/CCSSI_ELA%20Standards.pdf

Johnson, B. (2013). *Teaching students to dig deeper: The common core in action.* Larchmont, NY: Eye on Education.

Schmoker, M. (2011). *Focus: Elevating the essentials to radically improve student learning.* Alexandria, VA: Association of Supervision and Curriculum Development.

CHAPTER 7

Reading, Reading, Reading—But What About Writing?

Introduction: Two Peas in a Pod

I can by no means convey the importance of writing in the content areas in one chapter. However, I wouldn't feel right if I did not at least touch on the subject of writing in content area classes to meet the demands of the Common Core Standards. Often, writing is viewed as a way for students to demonstrate knowledge, which is true. However, I would also like for you to consider writing as a way for students to gain knowledge and to strengthen comprehension of content. Sousa (2011) states that "aspects of thinking include learning, memory, creativity, communication, logic, and generalization" (p. 251). These same aspects of thinking are included in the rewards of writing. The writing demands of the Common Core teacher are high, and the expectations are specific. This chapter will not be able to provide you with an elaborate plan for how to engage students in content writing in your classroom, but it will at least get you thinking about the possibilities!

When I first began my teaching career, I quickly learned how many assumptions I had wrong about student learning. I had a lovely group of 7th and 8th graders that first year and a very special girl named Chelsea. I loved Chelsea for many reasons, but one in particular was her love of reading! We would spend lunch periods talking about what we were reading and use one another's recommendations for what to read next. Chelsea was an A student, and I believed that her grades came rather easily to her in all of her classes. It wasn't until several months into the year, during our work on a narrative that she said to me, "I hate writing."

I was horrified.

"But . . . you love to read!" I stammered, I'm sure with terror and shock all over my face. She didn't seem to make the connection. "If you love reading, you should love writing!" I quickly informed her.

"Well, I don't," Chelsea insisted. "Writing takes too long, and it's boring." She didn't mean to be rude or malicious; she was just stating a simple fact. I'm sure I spent the rest of the period trying to convince her otherwise, but what I needed to do was show her the benefits and power of writing. I was used to kids telling me they hated to read, but how could this stellar student not like to write?

It took some years of experience for me to really understand how much of a challenge writing is for many of our students and, to my surprise, even for the strong readers like Chelsea. Also, unless you spend a lot of time looking at student writing, it can be difficult to tell how good or bad their writing is, whether created in a content area or for pleasure. Students have been trained to answer questions, like Pavlov's dogs. They can write in a structured format for questions and answers, but do we encourage them to write to truly demonstrate a comprehension of content or their own insightfulness? Do we encourage our students to use writing as a tool for learning or only as a task for presenting basic information?

This purpose of this chapter is to examine the relationship between purposeful writing and the English Language Arts Common Core Standards for History/Social Studies and Science and Technical Subjects. We will discuss using writing in the content area classroom as a tool for learning. Then, we will go on to look at ways students can use writing to strengthen comprehension through argument, information, explanation and research, all tools that are necessary to be successful in the 21st-century classroom and workforce. We spend a lot of time talking about how to make our students readers, so let's make sure they're writers as well! Let's begin our discussion on writing with how it can be used as a tool for learning!

Writing as Learning

Writing can serve many purposes: inviting someone to a dinner party, giving directions, asking for help, rallying support, communicating with a friend or providing information. But consider why people keep journals or diaries? What power is there in writing for reflection or for processing information or events? In our classrooms, writing is often underused as a tool for learning. Writing is not only a tool to demonstrate knowledge; it is a tool for learning and experimenting with new ideas or concepts. Robb (2003) states that "writing in the content areas is not a separate, optional activity, it is integral to the thinking process in social studies, science, and math" (p. 59).

Generally, when writing is used as a tool for learning, the work is done informally. Johnson (2013) states "when we write to learn, we analyze, we revise, we organize, we rewrite, we evaluate, and so on until what is written is what we want to communicate" (p. 132). When writing for learning, the end result should not be taken for a grade. Just as reading is a process, writing is its own process and should be treated similarly. You wouldn't expect your students to be experts after reading a chapter once, and the same is true for writing. Students can be asked to write to work through a process, making connections, comparisons or inferences, along with many other learning techniques. Sometimes writing is the missing piece that helps students make sense of an idea or concept. Writing helps students work through their learning step by step and find the information.

Students are familiar with the concept of brainstorming and should be taught to think of writing as learning in a similar way. Students should be aware that it will not be taken for a grade and be confident that there are no wrong answers. Writing is a way to generate ideas and thinking. When writing to learn, students should be given only a short period to write—for middle and high school students, no longer than 15 minutes. Students can be asked to observe and write a response, make predictions, summarize or respond to a content-related prompt.

Here's where I have to ask you to take a leap of faith. As I said, students should not be graded for this work. When you are walking around the room or writing with your students, here's a shocker: some of them will not be writing. They will be staring into space, doodling on their paper or looking to a friend for an answer. It's OK. Yes, it happens, and it's OK. Are some students not doing the assignment just because it's not for a grade? It's a possibility. Other students may simply have a more difficult time getting their ideas from brain to paper. I'm not saying to let them sit and do nothing, I'm saying let them sit and do nothing for a few minutes. Here's another confession: I'm a doodler. I know it drives my principal crazy in meetings, but I'm still listening! Some kids are thinking while their doodling; give them some time to work through their own processes from brain to paper. Remember, learning is a process.

To write, students must use their brains to think. Thinking strategies in this sense are writing strategies. Students should use their writing to think about working through a process, making connections, comparing and inferring. Again, consider the purpose when assigning writing activities; is it a task to demonstrate knowledge or a strategy to learn information? The purpose should determine whether and how the assignment is assessed. Writing for learning is not to demonstrate knowledge; it is to gain knowledge and strengthen understanding. For example, in working though a multistep process, students may be able to figure out a missing step by writing out the other steps they know, in order to see what's missing, for the information to make sense. If students are asked to brainstorm information, they can write down how they connected their thoughts to the content to see how things are related as a whole.

Writing a reflection is a wonderful tool for learning as well. We've discussed the power and importance of reflection in earlier chapters, but for students, writing is one of the strongest forms of reflecting on their own learning, understanding and outcomes. Writing a reflection on content is important to student learning because, unlike a summary, students may include their own thoughts and opinions incorporated with facts. Students may be asked to write a reflection after watching a video, experiment or lesson. Providing students with time to write and to reflect on how they learned a concept or the outcome of a unit, is a powerful learning strategy and gives students the opportunity to view learning as something that they can control and be a part of in order to achieve success.

Writing to Argue

The Common Core Standards for Writing in History/Social Studies or Science and Technical Subjects work progressively through grades 6–12. The first Standard for each grade band asks students to, "Write arguments focused on discipline-specific content." When students are demonstrating comprehension through argument writing, they are using a variety of higher-level thinking skills, including building defense, justifying, creating and evaluating. Argumentative writing may be used to try to persuade someone, defend a position or criticize someone else's position.

The first step in argument writing is selecting a topic. You can decide how topics will be assigned; all students may be writing on the same topic, they may have a choice of four or five topics or they may be allowed to select any topic approved by the teacher. It is crucial that the assignment is clearly tied to the content. Students need to understand the relationship and purpose of writing. Another question you should ask yourself before assigning argumentative writing is, "Will the students be able to argue only for the side they agree with on the topic?" If everyone in the class believes that the South should not have been allowed to secede from the Union, is it OK that they all write with that purpose? Or would it be somehow beneficial for some of your class to write for the opposing side? I personally believe that sometimes it can be beneficial for students to write as a devil's advocate and that it can help them look at the content more critically.

The Common Core Writing Standards begin by asking that students "write arguments focused on discipline-specific content" and then to get to the specifics in the subsections of the Standard. Let's take a look at the Standard in Table 7.1 and make sure we understand what it is asking of our students.

TABLE 7.1 Standard 1 for Writing in History/Social Studies or Science and Technical Subjects, Grades 6–8

Grades 6–8	Students Will . . .	Getting Students to the Standard
1. Write arguments focused on discipline-specific content.	Give reasons and evidence to support something or someone with the intention of defending, arguing or persuading the audience about the content.	During or after a unit on World War II, ask students to take a stand on the effectiveness of the United States' decisions following Pearl Harbor, citing reasoning and evidence from numerous texts.
1a. Introduce claims about a topic or issue, acknowledge and distinguish the claims from alternate or opposing claims, and organize the reasons and evidence logically.	Understand how to set up or organize an argumentative essay. (See Appendix A18, p. 157, for a model.)	Have students use graphic organizers to organize their information, and have them discuss the content and play devil's advocate before writing.
1b. Support claims with logical reasoning and relevant, accurate data and evidence that demonstrate an understanding of the topic or text, using credible sources.	Defend their opinions with text-based evidence and data to support their reasoning. Write to prove comprehension of content.	Ask students to write an outline of their argument without using any sources to see whether they can get from one point to the next. Argument should be based on student's own reasoning and then supported with sources. If they can, students should then find evidence and sources to back up their own reasoning and claims.
1c. Use words, phrases, and clauses to create cohesion and clarify the relationships among claims, counterclaims, reasons and evidence.	Write an argument that flows smoothly.	Help students organize their argument by using outlines or graphic organizers to help create a visual of how the argument will fit together. When they are editing, ask students to circle clauses and transition words.
1d. Establish and maintain a formal style.	Keep a continuous tone, style and mood throughout the paper that demonstrates formal writing.	Ask students to read their writing aloud. Discuss author's purpose and intended audience.
1e. Provide a concluding statement or section that follows from and supports the argument presented.	Wrap up the main points of their argument in a conclusion.	Students who can write summaries can usually write conclusions. Ask students to identify the key points of their argument and defend why each is a critical component of their paper.

Writing arguments is a great way to get students to demonstrate content knowledge and take that knowledge a step further by applying it to real-world situations and defending their own opinions. Argument writing may take your students some time to master because they're often not used to the freedom they're being given and voicing their own opinions. When I first began teaching argumentative writing, I had a frustrated student say to me, "You're the teacher. You're supposed to tell me what to think!" Our job is not to tell students what to think; our responsibility is to get them to think! The Common Core encourages a new way of presenting and demonstrating information, and in time we will get there for the good of our students and their futures.

Writing to Inform or Explain

The second Standard for Writing History/Social Studies or Science and Technical Subjects asks that students be able to write informative and explanatory texts. Unlike argument writing, this is a concept that our students are very familiar and often quite comfortable with. It is likely that your students complete some type of informatory or explanatory writing every day. Once again, it's up to you to decide how much time to spend on which topics and units you want to make into larger, lengthier and timelier writing assignments. Remember that writing is a form of learning, and decide on the best way for you and your students to use it. Look at the details and complexity of the Standard in Table 7.2.

Writing to inform and to explain can be a lengthy process, or it can be a quick five-minute activity. Students should be asked to complete both processes frequently as a way of demonstrating knowledge and learning information. Although the Writing History/Social Studies or Science and Technical Subjects Standards do not specifically discuss narrative writing, that does not mean they cannot be used in your classroom. For example, having your students write a narrative from the point of view of an atom or of Thomas Jefferson can be both informative and explanatory. As teachers, we have to be open-minded and take baby steps to get us where we need to be with our teaching and our students.

Writing for Research and Writing as a Process

The remaining English Language Arts Common Core Standards for Writing History/Social Studies or Science and Technical Subjects focus on process writing and research writing. Content area classrooms have been

TABLE 7.2 Standard 2 for Writing in History/Social Studies or Science and Technical Subjects, Grades 9–10

Standard	Students Will . . .	Getting Students to the Standard
2. Write informative/explanatory texts, including the narration of historical events, scientific experiments or technical processes.	Portray or explain information in a well written essay.	Teach students to identify key points, and frequently practice summarizing and outlining strategies.
2a. Introduce a topic and organize ideas, concepts, and information to make important connections and distinctions; include formatting (e.g. headings), graphics, and multimedia when useful to aiding comprehension.	Write an informative or explanatory essay that is clearly organized and formatted. Include graphics and multimedia when possible.	Ask students to prepare their information using graphic organizers or outlines. Analyze a variety of other texts on the same topic and discuss which graphics, formatting or multimedia would have added to student comprehension.
2b. Develop the topic with well-chosen, relevant, and sufficient facts, extended definitions, concrete details, quotations, or other information and examples appropriate to the audience's knowledge of the topic.	Display a deep understanding of the topic by referencing a variety of information and selecting relevant information and supporting details.	Ask, "Why?" Teach students the importance of backing up facts with more facts, and require them to use a wide variety of means, including quotes, texts, articles, journals, textbooks and videos. Spend class time analyzing and discussing strong versus weak information.
2c. Use varied transitions and sentence structures to link the major sections of the text, create cohesion, and clarify the relationships among ideas and concepts.	Write an informative or explanatory essay that flows smoothly and shows cohesion among ideas and relationships.	Expose your students to a variety of text structures including chronological, cause–effect, problem–solution and descriptive. Teach key words and phrases that can easily be incorporated with each structure. Encourage students to read written work aloud.

2d. Use precise language and domain-specific vocabulary to manage the complexity of the topic and convey a style appropriate to the discipline and context as well as to the expertise of likely readers.

Write in a complex style, using precise and content-rich vocabulary to convey information that is appropriate for their audience.

Expose students to a wide variety of content rich texts. Examine the differences between informal and formal writings and discuss the purposes for each, including how information is presented to the reader.

2e. Establish and maintain a formal style and objective tone while attending to the norms and conventions of the discipline in which they are writing.

Write in a formal and objective tone, considering the discipline in which they are writing.

Ask students to write a wide variety of texts and discuss when it is appropriate to include thoughts and opinions and when the writer must be objective. Discuss the purpose of different types of writing.

2f. Provide a concluding statement or section that follows from and supports the information or explanation presented (e.g., articulating implications or the significance of the topic).

Bring their ideas together in a strong, well organized conclusion that logically supports the information or explanation presented in their paper.

Have students practice writing one-sentence summaries. Trust me, it's much more difficult than it sounds!

completing research papers since the beginning of formal education; however, until recently, I believe that, for the most part, the writing process has been left behind in the English classroom. Let's take a look at both process writing and research writing a bit more closely.

What's important to understand about writing as a process is that every assignment will not be a drawn-out, edit-and-revise assignment. You will still get to choose how your students are learning and spending their time. This is not something that you will be doing every day, but it is important and significant that students are writing as a process in your content area. Completing a formal process of writing requires students to use many skills, including reflecting, organizing, planning and revising. Working and learning through a piece of writing is a multistep process and one of the most critical tools you can teach students to prepare them for college.

Most of our students are quite familiar with research writing and projects. Most students understand the concept of research and the concept of writing; the difficulty lies in putting the two concepts together without plagiarizing. Research writing is difficult for students and teachers, but remember that research can consist of hands-on learning as well as using text, digital technology, interviews and more. Once students can gather relevant information and organize it meaningfully, the transition to getting the information to paper will come much more easily. Let's take a look more closely at each Standard in detail in Table 7.3.

Writing is a critical tool that our students must be able to use effectively in order to be successful in their future careers or in college. Writing can be used as a thinking tool or as a way for students to demonstrate comprehension of content. The complexity of the writing and the way you choose to assign and use it depends on the content and goals of individual lessons, but I hope that you can find some way to get your students writing daily. Whether you are ready to jump right in and make writing a real focus in your classroom or you are going to work from baby steps to a nice, steady walk, you will see the difference in the quality of writing and in the way students demonstrate understanding of content.

TABLE 7.3 Common Core Standards 4–10 for Writing History/Social Studies or Science and Technical Subjects, Grades 11–12

Grades 11–12	Students Will . . .	Getting Students to the Standard
3. Produce clear and coherent writing in which the development, organization, and style are appropriate to task, purpose, and audience.	Create writings that are well organized, demonstrate understanding in content and show thoughtfulness for the task, purpose and audience.	Spend time discussing the role of author's purpose and intended audience with students and how they affect content area writing.
3a. Develop and strengthen writing as needed by planning, revising, editing, rewriting, or trying a new approach, focusing on addressing what is most significant for a specific purpose and audience.	Write as a process: plan, revise, edit, rewrite or, if necessary, take a different approach to the content.	Break longer and more formal writing assignments down into steps that students can work through at their own pace.
3b. Use technology, including the Internet, to produce, publish, and update individual or shared writing products in response to ongoing feedback, including new arguments or information.	Use technology to strengthen their writing by producing and publishing online and by using audience feedback to update written work. Become familiar with a large variety of online sites and apps that students can use to blog, share written work, create storyboards, and hold discussions.	Teach students to be thoughtful critics. Saying, "It's good" or "I don't like it" isn't thoughtful. Students should consider supporting documentation, organization, tone and other elements to provide a thoughtful critique. At first, it may be beneficial for students to use a critiquing rubric when responding to a peer's written work.
3c. Conduct short as well as more sustained research projects to answer a question (including a self-generated question) or solve a problem; narrow or broaden the inquiry when appropriate; synthesize multiple sources on the subject, demonstrating understanding of the subject under investigation.	Answer questions or solve a problem through research. When researching and writing the inquiry should be appropriate to the content, use several sources and prove comprehension of the content.	Stop giving students the answer! Encourage them to learn through inquiry-based projects to find answers and solve problems. Present research as a quest for answers, not a boring copy session of restating someone else's ideas.

(*Continued*)

TABLE 7.3 (Continued)

Grades 11–12	Students Will . . .	Getting Students to the Standard
3d. Gather relevant information from multiple authoritative print and digital sources, using advanced searches effectively; assess the strengths and limitations of each source in terms of the specific task, purpose, and audience; integrate information into the text selectively to maintain the flow of ideas, avoiding plagiarism and overreliance on any one source and following a standard format for citation.	Understand what constitutes as a strong or weak source, considering task, purpose and audience. Students select sources that add character to their paper and its flow without plagiarizing or relying on one text too heavily for information. Students will accurately cite their sources.	Require students to use a specific number and variety of sources and to expose them to rich sources within the content. Analyze the validity and strength of various sources in small groups to ensure that each student can find strengths and weaknesses within a print or digital source.
3e. Draw evidence from informational texts to support analysis, reflection, and research.	Use a wide variety of texts to support analysis, reflection and research.	Teach students numerous ways to support their writing; direct quotes, examples and similar findings.
3f. Write routinely over extended time frames (time for reflection and revision) and shorter time frames (a single sitting or a day or two) for a range of discipline-specific tasks, purposes, and audiences.	Adapt their writing to fit the needs and purpose of a given task, considering the content, purpose and audience.	Require that students write often for a variety of audiences and a variety of purposes.

Review: What to Do, What to Do!

- Use writing to strengthen student comprehension of content.
- Writing can be a tool or strategy for learning content.
- Be sure that students understand the purpose and process of writing before they begin to work.
- Teach students various forms of writing, including argumentative, informative and explanatory. Use each of these forms often and in various degrees.
- Explain to students that good research leads to great writing.
- Encourage students to think of reading and writing as a happily married couple, each bringing out the best in the other.

References

Common Core State Standards Initiative. (2010). *Common core state standards for English language arts literacy in history/social studies, science, and technical subjects.* Washington, DC: National Governors Association Center for Best Practices and Council of Chief State School Officers. Retrieved March 5, 2013 from www.corestandards.org/assets/CCSSI_ELA%20Standards.pdf

Johnson, B. (2013). *Teaching students to dig deeper: The common core in action.* Larchmont, NY: Eye on Education.

Robb, L. (2003). *Teaching reading in social studies, science, and math: Practical ways to weave comprehension strategies into your content area teaching.* New York: Scholastic.

Sousa, D. A. (2011). *How the brain learns* (4th ed.). Thousand Oaks, CA: Corwin.

CHAPTER

Projects, Grading and Literacy? Is This More Work for Me?

Introduction: Swimming in Quicksand

I love my job . . . most of the time. However, I'm not going to say that, at the end of the day, I've never felt like putting my head down on my desk and crying. It happens. Teachers are busy, and we never get to enjoy that feeling of being caught up. The work is never done; it's like laundry but worse. When I have stacks of papers to grade, midterms to enter, lessons to plan, parents to call and students to help, it's all I can do to keep from silently weeping in my hands when my principal tells me we're starting something new. According to Eyster and Martin (2010):

> All of us who have come to care about our students and our colleagues and even our schools know that there is quicksand potential in our commitment to our jobs. Until three o'clock, we are giving ourselves to our students, to the photocopy machine, to conferences about the child with cancer-stricken father, and after three o'clock—often long after—we are still similarly occupied, grading papers, writing tests, drafting lesson plans. (p. 256)

With all that we do and the many amazing things we accomplish, it's only normal that at times we feel overwhelmed. Feeling overwhelmed is scary for teachers because we care about our students. We don't want to have to sacrifice the things we know are important to meet a new trend in education. Here's the thing: sometimes the trend is something good.

Education doesn't stay the same; it's like an evolving, living creature. Change is hard and can feel a bit overwhelming, but wouldn't you get bored doing the same things every year? When laws, Standards, testing, procedures and our students seem to be changing on a yearly basis—or at times a daily basis—we can feel as though we're swimming in quicksand, trying so hard to get somewhere but not moving. As educators, we know what we need to do, but the question is, as it is so often, how do I get where I need to be?

Balancing content area teaching, projects, inquiry-based learning, grading and literacy may make you feel as though you're carrying the weight of the world on your back. However, teachers are like ants. Ants can carry 10–15% of their body weight, and most teachers could give ants a run for their money. Teachers are pro's at rolling with the punches. New terminology, assessments and laws make it seem like a whole new profession at times, when really our ultimate goal is the same: help students grow academically and prepare them for college and career and become contributing members of society. This chapter's goal is to give you some muscle to help you carry the weight of being an effective teacher.

Initially, change can mean more work for teachers, but anytime you try something new, work is involved, and work often leads to rewards. The change is scary, and the rewards may not be immediate, but with the Common Core Standards we will see our students reap the benefits of our hard work. This chapter will discuss how, with a little change, we can balance the demands of our profession. We will discuss how doing less can sometimes equal doing more; how to use time wisely when time is indeed so precious; how to make the most of grading, planning to meet the needs of our students and the demands of the Common Core; and how collaboration may just save the day for teachers.

The Release of Power

I have the luxury of working with one of the most fabulous special education inclusion teachers on the planet. That being said, it's taken me a lot of time to let a coteacher shine their light on me. Here's the thing: I'm a control freak. I want things done my way. I'm a spoiled, whiny brat in a grown woman's body. I like having things done my way because I am passionate about what I do and put a lot of time and effort into making things the best that I can for me and my students. I'm sure you have done the same. Unfortunately, that can make teachers, let's say . . . touchy. How can a group of adults who work with children and teens every day be so sensitive? Once again, we care so much about what we do that even the slightest recommendation or comment can bring anger or tears. In today's state of education, it's hard not to feel as though everyone in the world is telling us how to do our job. Yet, believe it or not, sometimes criticism is good, and sometimes people really are just trying to be helpful.

I've learned that one of the best ways to feel less overwhelmed and become more effective is actually to do less. Sounds counterproductive, right? Here's why doing less works. Other people have good ideas too, and their giving you an idea doesn't mean they're taking anything away from the way you're doing something. For example, perhaps you know the feeling of anxiety you get before you meet your student teacher. Will your classroom be turned upside down while you babysit one extra person? Or will you use it as an opportunity to learn new things? You've heard of helicopter parents, hovering over their children everywhere they go? I used to be a helicopter teacher. Things were my way or the highway. I would allow student teachers into my classroom but micromanage every aspect of their experience. I couldn't bring myself to give up control, even though every student teacher I have had the pleasure to work with and mentor has been outstanding.

Over the years of working with so many wonderful people, teachers and students, I've finally learned to trust everyone a little more. Trusting others is the first step in giving up control. Here's another thing to consider. What's the worst thing that could happen? You have one bad lesson or one bad day. Don't you have those days yourself? In a Common Core Classroom, giving up some of the power will benefit you and your students. Balancing projects, grading and literacy are a lot for teachers to do on their own. You don't have to, so relax!

The power or control given to coteachers and even student teachers allows you to have more time to work individually with students, create lesson plans, complete grading or grow professionally through reading or observing new practices. If you have an inclusion teacher in your classroom one or five periods a day, find a way to use him or her effectively for the sake of your students. With the literacy demands of the Common Core Standards, there will hopefully be much more reading and writing in your classroom. Allow your classroom to become a true inclusion setting by creating lesson plans together, sharing the responsibility of grading and working interactively in small group settings. Most inclusion teachers really want to do more in the classroom, but it's hard for us to give up our power! Use the Common Core as an opportunity to do new things and renew your enthusiasm for teaching.

Here's another way to give up some of your control: give the power to your students! According to Johnson (2013), "students and teachers working together can achieve substantial learning gains. Teachers working by themselves will achieve nothing" (p. 119). To be college and career ready, students will need to learn to take control of their own successes and failures. The Common Core Standards call for inquiry-based learning, collaboration and the use of technology. Although it's a little scary, our ultimate goal is that our students will need us less and less as they take control of their learning.

As far as inquiry-based projects, students should really be creating their own questions and finding their own resources. Obviously, the majority of your work will come in preparation and anticipation of the project. If you have a well organized plan for projects in advance, the time spent working on projects in and out of class should be student centered. During this time, you will act more as a monitor, coach, resource and helper. I recommend enforcing an ask-another-first rule, whereby students must ask another student or member of their group for help before asking you. It's important to emphasize that our classrooms are teams and that all students are learning and collaborating. Enforcing such a rule gives you more time to monitor that students are on task, to coach and scaffold students in the right direction through discussion and resources and to help the groups or students that truly need assistance, not answers.

Giving up control of your grading is another scary scenario for teachers, especially the idea of giving students the power to grade. When we talk about giving our students the power to grade, we're talking about giving students the opportunity to take control of their learning. I'm not saying to ask students whether they deserve an A or an F and be done with it but to give students the chance to thoughtfully reflect on their work. Teachers should take students' reflections into consideration and spend time discussing grading procedures with them, ultimately spending less time trying to decipher who did what and how students reached an end result.

Although at times it may feel like you've lost all control, you make the decisions in your classroom. You get to decide what you are ready to give up, what you want to teach and how much you can handle—and, let's face it, some days you can handle more than others. You have the power to decide how much time is spent strictly on content area learning, how to incorporate literacy and how much help you're going to accept. In my experience, giving up some of your power just might make you more powerful.

Time Management

It's not easy being a teacher. Some days I don't get a minute to myself to think until lunch, and on those days I don't spend my lunch checking e-mail, grading papers or planning lessons. I'm pretty sure that most of the world believes that teachers get off work at 3:30 p.m. and spend the rest of their day, along with their summers, watching television, traveling the world and frolicking like an unemployed college student.

We know the truth. When we get home from work, we spend as much time as we can with family and complete the necessities that make each of our worlds go round, then we return to teaching mode—grading, planning and more grading. During the summer, sure we go to the pool, but we also complete endless hours of professional development, take classes on a graduate level, read professional texts, collaborate with our peers and plan for the following year, not to mention getting our classrooms in order.

Obviously, some teachers manage their time better than others, but we can all do a few things to help us use our time effectively: don't grade everything, plan ahead with unit planning and then with daily planning, get organized (make lists), delegate jobs and responsibilities, collaborate with content area teachers, get on a schedule and prioritize. I understand that everyone does things differently, and, just like our students, we have to find what works best on an individual level. However, while learning and implementing the Common Core Standards, some of these strategies can be quite helpful and worth considering.

We're going to talk more about grading next, but with a focus on literacy, inquiry-based learning and projects for which you may have to approach grading a little differently. Here's the thing that we know, but for some reason feel guilty about: you don't have to grade everything. In a score-driven world, it can be difficult to justify to our students what and how we grade and convince them that work is often for their own benefit, not a point value. However, grading everything in detail will quickly bury you while implementing new literacy heavy Standards. I recommend grading finished products only, not every step. It is important to monitor students while they're working and keep the lines of communication open, but grade only the finished product. It is also OK to walk around the room to grade informally, perhaps picking a single question to check or one sentence to read, to ensure that students are getting the big ideas. Also, just because you are now more than ever a literacy teacher doesn't mean that you need to start marking spelling errors, grammatical problems and other English concepts on every assignment. Focus on the content and then prioritize other concepts for large assignments or projects.

Planning and time management are key to a successful classroom. It is crucial to student learning that teachers know the focus of the unit before beginning and how and when they will ask students to demonstrate knowledge. We will talk more about planning later in the chapter. Combining what we already have and use with new content and new literacy Standards calls for good organization. Teachers are going to have to make connections between their content Standards and English Language Arts Common Core Standards, it is important to find a way to keep everything straight that works for you, whether it's through checklists, online sources or data folders.

We've already discussed giving up some of your power, which is also a time management strategy. Believe it or not, at times (very few), you cannot do it all on your own. Make better use of your time by delegating jobs and responsibilities. I don't mean push your work off on other people, but think about the things you do every day that have nothing to do with the success of your students. Many students are always looking to help a teacher and can be trusted with classroom jobs. As upper-level teachers, we have been trained to believe that classroom helpers are for elementary schools, but I think older students can be great helpers and can handle even more for us! Initially, delegating jobs can be time–consuming, but it saves us time and energy once students are trained for their work. Possible jobs that could be delegated to students are attendance taker, posting objectives on the board, paper monitor (collects and hands back papers) and homework monitor (deals with absent work).

For me, the biggest time management tool is my group of content area teachers. Through collaboration, I spend a lot less time creating new materials, units and strategies. Collectively, we create units, lessons, assessments and tools. I have no idea how I would create a year's worth of resources and lessons on my own, especially while we're learning new Standards. As a group, we work on almost the same schedule. Scheduling events, lessons and activities is also important for time management and can be beneficial for our students so that they know what to expect. When you are dealing with time and that nagging overwhelmed feeling, all you can do is prioritize. Some days things just have to wait, and that's OK. Decide what you can do and what is most important to you and the success of your students, and go with it!

Grading

Grading is crucial to student learning and teaching. Through grading, teachers learn what their students have mastered, what they need to reteach, when students are ready to move on and how students can most effectively demonstrate knowledge. In a perfect world, students would examine their grades and use their scores and feedback to analyze their own strengths and weaknesses and to decide how to improve or grow as learners. However, with 100–150 students, grading everything can be quite a goal to accomplish. Grading is a lot of work and takes up a lot of precious time that we could spend working with our students and creating masterful lessons. Here's the thing: in our grade-driven state of education, they are quite the necessity. I wish I could tell you that grades are not necessary and that students should simply work to learn. Wouldn't that be nice! Well, I can't tell you that, but I can tell you a few things to help you carry the weight of grading, including grading less, conferencing with your students, grading by Standard, grading with a focus and creating a system to handle student work.

We have talked about grading less and how sometimes less is more. Unfortunately, if our students know that something is not worth points, they can't see the value in completing the assignment. In our grade-driven world, I can hardly blame them. That being said, you still don't need to grade everything, or at least you don't need to grade everything for complete accuracy. If you're asking students to read and respond, give checkmarks or stamps for completion. At the end of the grading period or once a month, ask students to turn in three stamped assignments for points. When working with larger assignments or lengthy projects, explain to students that each step is a progressive learning tool to master the end result.

We spend a lot of time talking to our students. We discuss sports, content being covered in class, what they did over the weekend, school drama and more, but how much time do you spend discussing grades with them? Now, "discussing grades" is not students asking you what their grade is and you responding. I am talking about a thoughtful conversation with feedback on grades and their direct connection to student learning. Taking the time to conference with students individually may sound impossible, but if you make it a priority and conference with a specific focus, it's worth it. Most of you have 25–30 students each class period. I recommend meeting with students once every two weeks to discuss grades in a three-minute conference. I like to keep a stopwatch or timer on my desk that the student and I can both watch. Conference time must also be scheduled into your lessons. You can meet with five students in 15 minutes each period while the class is completing their reading, working on an assignment or doing group work. What would be most effective in your classroom? Once you begin student grading conferences, you will need to stay focused to complete them in three minutes. I like to have a printout of each student's grade broken down for the student and me to look at together. During the conference, the focus is to answer three basic questions. Are you happy with the grade you have? Do you feel it accurately portrays what you know? How can you improve your grade or grow as a learner or be challenged? Talking with students meaningfully about their grades helps them see the importance of what they're doing, that you care about their learning and hopefully that they have control of their own success.

Other strategies to keep grading meaningful and under control are to grade by Standard and to grade with specific focus. Grading by Standard will help you see how individual students progress and analyze their strengths and weaknesses. That being said, I realize that most assignments, projects and tests cover numerous Standards. You will have to make a judgment call to see whether you can either select one main Standard to focus on or perhaps split the assignment into more than one category. I think that the most effective way to view how students progress through each Standard is to set up your grade book by Standard instead of by types of assignment. Often, we break our grade book down into sections like homework, tests, quizzes, projects and the like. I would break your grading into sections by Standard to enable you and your students to easily view where their strengths and weaknesses lie.

The most important part of grading is to create an effective system that works for you and your students so as to handle their assignments and to track student learning in a meaningful way. Whether you make the baby step of posting grades weekly or run ahead to biweekly conferences is up to you, but it is crucial, when readying students for college and career, to include them in the grading process and to teach them that they are responsible for the outcome of their work and grades. Grading is one thing that teachers are never really caught up on, or if you are, the celebration doesn't last long. Just remember that it's OK for grading to work like a revolving door; just don't put so much through the door that it gets jammed!

Planning

Planning. Whether you love it or hate it, it must be done! As an admitted control freak and organizer, I love planning. The gathering of materials, figuring out what my kids really know, discussing which strategies and learning tools will work best or be most helpful are all some of my favorite aspects of teaching! In Chapter 2 we began to talk about how unit planning is critical to success with the Common Core Standards. Unit planning is the ground on which your daily plans will be built. Gallagher (2004) states that "assessment should drive the teaching. When teacher and students know the assessment beforehand, more focused teaching and learning will result" (p. 209). We need a focused unit and lesson with specific goals to lead us to effective teaching and learning. Unit planning enables teachers to tie concepts together and easily analyze where students are coming from and the direction in which they need to head. Solid unit planning makes daily planning less overwhelming. Wiggins and McTighe (2005) state:

> Many educators have observed that backward design is common sense. Yet when we first start to apply it, they discover that it feels unnatural. Working this way may seem a bit awkward and time-consuming until you get the hang of it. But the effort is worth it—just as the learning curve on good soft-ware is worth it. (p. 21)

A unit plan will clearly lay out the purpose of what you're teaching, whereas the daily lesson plans will get into the detail of how you're going to reach the desired end results.

The unit plan in Chapter 3 is a great starting point and can also be found in Appendix A8 (p. 139).

When working on daily plans, you will need to constantly go back to your unit plan to stay focused on the main learning goals and purposes. While the unit plan focuses on English Language Arts Common Core Standards, the daily plans should be specific outlines of how your classroom flows: content focus, writing activities, reading activities, primary and secondary sources, speaking and listening activities, projects, multimedia and visual information, formative and summative assessments, possible enrichment and critical thinking questions.

Using your unit plan as a guide, I recommend incorporating the following aspects into your daily lesson plans: goal(s), objectives, activities ("students will," "teacher will"), materials and evaluation procedure(s). As I've said, I'm not a fan of three-page lesson plans, and, more importantly, I do not think they are at all realistic for working teachers. But I do believe that it's important to have a plan, a purpose and a goal for working with students. Figure 8.1 shows a possible weekly planning page to build from your unit plan. Or if you like working on a longer timescale, you can view your lessons weekly, as shown in Figure 8.2.

Teacher:		Subject:	Unit:	Date:
Day:	Goal(s):	Activities		Materials:
		Students will	Teacher will	
	Objectives:			
				Evaluation Procedure(s):

FIGURE 8.1 Lesson Planning

Each of the main components of the lesson plan has a specific purpose and should be easily related to the unit plan. Let's look at each section.

- *Goal(s):* These are the big ideas or broad objectives. Goals, gathered from the unit planning guide, should be the focus.
- *Objectives:* Specific, attainable and concrete statements of what the students will be able to do during or after the lesson.
- *Activities:* ("students will," "teacher will"): Activities are not just for students. Ask yourself what you will be doing while students are reading, completing group work or other tasks. Be sure to include an approximate time for each task.

	Teacher:	Subject:	Unit:	Date:	
	Goal(s):	Activities		Materials:	
		Students will	Teacher will		
Monday					
	Objectives:				
				Evaluation Procedure(s):	
	Goal(s):	Activities		Materials:	
		Students will	Teacher will		
Tuesday					
	Objectives:				
				Evaluation Procedure(s):	
	Goal(s):	Activities		Materials:	
		Students will	Teacher will		
Wednesday					
	Objectives:				
				Evaluation Procedure(s):	

FIGURE 8.2 Lesson Planning; Weekly Option

	Goal(s):	Activities		Materials:
Thursday		Students will	Teacher will	
	Objectives:			Evaluation Procedure(s):
Friday	Goal(s):	Activities		Materials:
		Students will	Teacher will	
	Objectives:			Evaluation Procedure(s):

FIGURE 8.2 (Continued)

- *Materials:* Based on the unit plan, you should have a general idea of the various sources you will be using throughout the time frame.
- *Evaluation procedure(s):* How will students show you what they have learned and their level of mastery?

Depending on how you plan your lessons, planning can be the life vest that carries you through the sand you're swimming in. Yet even if you have a plan, you must be flexible. Things happen, and sometimes lessons just don't flow as planned. But if you keep a general focus and purpose, you will always be working toward the same goal or end result. Wiggins and McTighe (2005) state that "achieving goals requires a carefully thought-out design, but we can usually only achieve our goals by deviating from the plan, in response to the considerable feedback and teachable moments that will occur in class" (p. 270). Managing projects, grading and literacy in a content area classroom require a solid plan, purpose and learning goal.

Collaboration

You've heard the phrase, "it takes a village . . . ." Well, that couldn't be more true for teachers. To be successful, we need the help of administrators, parents, family, peers and students. We can't do it all on our own, although often we try. When working with new Standards, assessments and students, collaboration is the key. If you want to make your life easier and your teaching better, I recommend collaborating with inclusion teachers, teachers in your own content area and teachers in other content areas in order to make the most of your time and energy.

If you teach in an inclusive setting, you probably understand how knowledgeable special education teachers are on differentiating and monitoring student's strengths and weaknesses. Even if you don't currently teach inclusion, these teachers are a great resource for certain situations. The English Language Arts Common Core Standards have students collaborating, completing projects and using inquiry-based learning, meaning that all of your students aren't going to be moving or learning at the same pace. You will have to be flexible with how students learn and find a variety of materials and resources for different learners. This is one way inclusion teachers can be very helpful. They can help you figure out which sources, texts and materials may be right for different types of learners and which may be best for students to display their knowledge. If you need help creating an environment that's flexible or working with different types of learning at the same time, ask a certified special education teacher for help!

Teachers in your shared content area can likely save you more time and energy than anyone else. Sacrificing one planning period each week or meeting before or after school for 30–40 minutes could save you hours in planning or creating materials. The benefits of working with other content area teachers are endless: planning together will help you create better and more effective lessons. Work can be divided, materials can be adapted or modified to meet the individual needs of students and data can be collected and shared to analyze where teacher and student strengths and weaknesses fall.

What I love most about the Common Core Standards is how they enable teachers from all content areas to work together. We must be collaborative models for our students. Gallagher (2004) states that "we know there is power in collaboration, and that even proficient readers can benefit greatly from the insight of others. Students need to discover this power as well" (p, 123). If you're going to be working with inquiry-based projects for the first time, find a science teacher! If you're dealing with reading and writing more than ever before, find an English teacher! If you're looking at how to analyze data and show student growth, find a math teacher! If you're struggling with getting kids to dig deeper into a lesson or make connections to text, find a social studies teacher! If you have the opportunity to work on a team, you can do big things with the Common Core that could include numerous content areas. How far you want to reach is really up to you. Don't try to do it all on your own.

Review: What to Do, What to Do!

- Don't be a control freak! You don't have to be in charge of everything for your classroom to run smoothly. Let the wonderful people around you help.
- Delegate jobs and responsibilities.
- Make the most of your time by being prepared.
- Don't feel as though you have to grade everything.
- Make time to conference with your students about grades and learning.
- Spending the time to plan will save you time.
- Collaborate with students and teachers. Don't try to do everything on your own. Your peers are your greatest resource.

References

Eyster, R. H., and Martin, C. (2010). *Successful classroom management.* Naperville, IL: Sourcebooks.

Gallagher, K. (2004). *Deeper reading: Comprehending challenging texts, 4–12.* Portland, ME: Stenhouse Publishers.

Johnson, B. (2013). *Teaching students to dig deeper: The common core in action.* Larchmont, NY: Eye on Education.

Wiggins, G., & McTighe, J. (2005). *Understanding by design* (2nd ed.). Alexandria, VA: Association for Supervision and Curriculum Development.

CHAPTER 9

There Is *No* Finish Line

The Conclusion: Why You're Awesome

As with all things in education, there is no easy way to wrap up this book. With teaching, there will never be an ultimate solution—"Well, that's it! This is the answer. Now go on your way." Answers don't fit into a neatly wrapped box. They come in something like a sloppy gift bag with scrunched-up tissue paper and the edge of the surprise peeking out. Luckily, the gift is just as good either way it comes. That's what we need to constantly remind ourselves: it's the end result that matters.

I hope this book made you realize that what you're already doing is great! I also hope it made you realize that things can always get better and that sometimes a simple adaption is all it takes. You are not starting over. You work hard, and at times you may feel unappreciated, but focus on the good and move past the bad. No one can be perfect. Even Superman has his weaknesses.

In conclusion, we will discuss balancing content and literacy in a Common Core classroom, how professional development and professional organizations can be beneficial and, finally, walking on your own and how things do get easier. The goal of this book is not change but progress, and we each progress at our own speed. I don't expect you to take off running toward a Common Core classroom, but I hope you are at least ready to walk in that direction.

Balancing Content and Literacy

Teaching the Common Core in the content areas will be a big change for some educators and a simple change for others. Our classrooms all run differently. The Common Core Standards strongly emphasize literacy, but don't let that make you feel as though your content is any less important. Content and literacy fit together perfectly. All you need to do is ask yourself four questions.

1. How can I teach this content through reading?
2. How can I teach this content through writing?
3. How will my students demonstrate knowledge of content through reading?
4. How will my students demonstrate knowledge of content writing?

Content and literacy cannot be separated no matter how hard you try. Finding the perfect balance may be difficult, but, with the help of the Common Core Standards, you will be able to see the connections between content and literacy and likely be teaching with more focus. According to Schmoker (2011), we need three basic strategies:

> Adequate amounts of essential subject-area content, concepts and topics; intellectual/thinking skills; and authentic literacy—purposeful reading, writing, and discussion as the primary modes of learning both content and thinking skills. (p. 26)

That doesn't sound so hard, right? Keep on doin' what you're doin'!

Professional Development

Here's my last confession: I hate meetings—all meetings, even when they're necessary. My antipathy is a result of sitting through too many meetings and professional development sessions that were by no means necessary. I really need to change my attitude. According to Johnson (2013), "teachers who are solely practitioners are confined to what knowledge and skills are currently within their experience" (p. 143). I was hurting myself and my students by being so close-minded. Luckily, many speakers have swayed me to their side and now have my full attention, through fantastic and worthwhile information and knowledge. Regardless of my best efforts, sometimes people just wow me.

As teachers, we will always have to attend meetings that make us feel as though we'd rather be having a root canal. It happens. Luckily, as teachers, we have the opportunity to pick much of our own professional development. According to Stover, Kissel, Haag and Shoniker (2011), "for meaningful change to occur, teachers must have a voice in the process of their own learning" (p. 499). Instead of just taking a class to complete the required hours, ask yourself, "What do I really need to work on? What would I like to know? What could I learn that would benefit the students I work with every day?" I promise you something is out there that will make you a better teacher!

The first step in finding good professional development opportunities is becoming a part of a professional organization. Unfortunately, teaching organizations are dying, and it's a shame because it's empowering to be a part of something we believe in. As a member and past president of the Ohio Council of Teachers of English Language Arts, I have grown as an educator and have became an advocate for what I do every day. The conference we hold every year is created by teachers, for teachers. I highly encourage you to find a national or state professional organization related to your content area, where you can learn and collaborate with people like you. Like our students, we can always learn something.

Rolling to Crawling to Baby Steps to Walking to Running: Things Get Easier

I like to be challenged, although sometimes it would just be nice for everything to be easy—to have a day when everything goes my way. Teaching certainly has its ups and downs. We have good years and not so good years, good months and not so good months and good days and not so good days. My nonteacher husband will never understand why September and May are so hectic. I guess you have to live it to understand it. Learning new things can be tough, and trying new things can be intimidating. But remember what it was like to be a first-year teacher. Oh, how far you've come! You may not be running every day, but I'm sure you're moving right along. That's progress.

Review: What to Do, What to Do!

- Keep on keepin' on!
- Balance content and literacy through effective planning. Spend time reflecting on what is important.
- Don't give up on finding worthwhile professional development.
- Consider joining a local, state or national professional organization.
- Teaching is not a sprint to the finish line; it's a marathon. The goal is progress.

References

Johnson, B. (2013). *Teaching students to dig deeper: The common core in action*. Larchmont, NY: Eye on Education.

Schmoker, M. (2011). *Focus: Elevating the essentials to radically improve student learning*. Alexandria, VA: Association of Supervision and Curriculum Development.

Stover, K., Kissel, B., Haag, K., and Shoniker, R. (2011). Differentiated coaching: Fostering reflection with teachers. *The Reading Teacher* 64 (7), 498–509.

APPENDIX

What You're Already Doing in History/Social Studies for Grades 6–8

TABLE A1 History/Social Studies, Grades 6–8

Standard	What You're Already Doing
1. Cite specific textual evidence to support analysis of primary and secondary sources.	
2. Determine the central ideas or conclusions of a text; provide an accurate summary of the text distinct from prior knowledge or opinions.	
3. Identify key steps in a text's description of a process related to history/social studies.	
4. Determine the meaning of words and phrases as they are used in a text, including vocabulary specific to domains related to history/social studies.	

5. Describe how a text presents information (e.g., sequentially, comparatively, causally).	
6. Identify aspects of a text that reveal an author's point of view or purpose (e.g., loaded language, inclusion or avoidance of particular facts).	
7. Integrate visual information (e.g., in charts, graphs, photographs, videos, or maps) with other information in print and digital texts.	
8. Distinguish among fact, opinion, and reasoned judgment in a text.	
9. Analyze the relationship between a primary and secondary source on the same topic.	
10. By the end of grade 8, read and comprehend history/social studies texts in the grades text complexity band independently and proficiently.	

APPENDIX

What You're Already Doing in History/Social Studies for Grades 9–10

TABLE A2 History/Social Studies, Grades 9–10

Grades 9–10	What You're Already Doing
Cite specific textual evidence to support analysis of primary and secondary sources, attending to such features as the date and origin of the information.	
Determine the central ideas or information of a primary or secondary source; provide an accurate summary of how key events or ideas develop over the course of the text.	
Analyze in detail a series of events described in a text; determine whether earlier events caused later ones or simply preceded them.	
Determine the meaning of words and phrases as they are used in a text, including vocabulary describing political, social, or economic aspects of history/social science.	

Analyze how a text uses structure to emphasize key points or advance an explanation or analysis.	
Compare the point of view of two or more authors for how they treat the same or similar topics, including which details they include and emphasize in their respective accounts.	
Integrate quantitative or technical analysis (e.g., charts, research data) with qualitative analysis in print or digital text.	
Assess the extent to which the reasoning and evidence in a text support the author's claims.	
Compare and contrast treatments of the same topic in several primary and secondary sources.	
By the end of grade 10, read and comprehend history/social studies texts in the grades 9–10 text complexity band independently and proficiently.	

APPENDIX

What You're Already Doing in History/Social Studies for Grades 11–12

TABLE A3 History/Social Studies Grades, 11–12

Grades 11–12	What You're Already Doing
Cite specific textual evidence to support analysis of primary and secondary sources, connecting insights gained from specific details to an understanding of the text as a whole.	
Determine the central ideas or information of a primary or secondary source; provide an accurate summary that makes clear the relationships among the key details and ideas.	
Evaluate various explanations for actions or events and determine which explanation best accords with textual evidence, acknowledging where the text leaves matters uncertain.	
Determine the meaning of words and phrases as they are used in a text, including analyzing how an author uses and refines the meaning of a key term over the course of a text (e.g., how Madison defines *faction* in *Federalist* No. 10).	

Analyze in detail how a complex primary source is structured, including how key sentences, paragraphs, and larger portions of the text contribute to the whole.	
Evaluate authors' differing points of view on the same historical event or issue by assessing the authors' claims, reasoning, and evidence.	
Integrate and evaluate multiple sources of information presented in diverse formats and media (e.g., visually, quantitatively, as well as in words) in order to address a question or solve a problem.	
Evaluate an author's premises, claims, and evidence by corroborating or challenging them with other information.	
Integrate information from diverse sources, both primary and secondary, into a coherent understanding of an idea or event, noting discrepancies among sources.	
By the end of grade 12, read and comprehend history/social studies texts in the grades 11–CCR text complexity band independently and proficiently.	

APPENDIX

What You're Already Doing in Science and Technical Subjects for Grades 6–8

TABLE A4 Science and Technical Subjects, Grades 6–8

Grades 6–8	What You're Already Doing
Cite specific textual evidence to support analysis of science and technical texts.	
Determine the central ideas or conclusions of a text; provide an accurate summary of the text distinct from prior knowledge or opinions.	
Follow precisely a multistep procedure when carrying out experiments, taking measurements, or performing technical tasks.	
Determine the meaning of symbols, key terms, and other domain-specific words and phrases as they are used in a specific scientific or technical context relevant to *grades 6–8 texts and topics*.	

© 2014 Taylor & Francis

Analyze the structure an author uses to organize a text, including how the major sections contribute to the whole and to an understanding of the topic.	
Analyze the author's purpose in providing an explanation, describing a procedure, or discussing an experiment in a text.	
Integrate quantitative or technical information expressed in words in a text with a version of that information expressed visually (e.g., in a flowchart, diagram, model, graph, or table).	
Distinguish among facts, reasoned judgment based on research findings, and speculation in a text.	
Compare and contrast the information gained from experiments, simulations, video, or multimedia sources with that gained from reading a text on the same topic.	
By the end of grade 8, read and comprehend science/technical texts in the grades 6–8 text complexity band independently and proficiently.	

APPENDIX

What You're Already Doing in Science and Technical Subjects for Grades 9–10

TABLE A5 Science and Technical Subjects Grades, 9–10

Grades 9–10	What You're Already Doing
Cite specific textual evidence to support analysis of science and technical texts, attending to the precise details of explanations or descriptions.	
Determine the central ideas or conclusions of a text; trace the text's explanation or depiction of a complex process, phenomenon, or concept; provide an accurate summary of the text.	
Follow precisely a complex multistep procedure when carrying out experiments, taking measurements, or performing technical tasks, attending to special cases or exceptions defined in the text.	
Determine the meaning of symbols, key terms, and other domain-specific words and phrases as they are used in a specific scientific or technical context relevant to *grades 9–10 texts and topics*.	

© 2014 Taylor & Francis

Analyze the structure of the relationships among concepts in a text, including relationships among key terms (e.g., *force, friction, reaction force, energy*).	
Analyze the author's purpose in providing an explanation, describing a procedure, or discussing an experiment in a text, defining the question the author seeks to address.	
Translate quantitative or technical information expressed in words in a text into visual form (e.g., a table or chart) and translate information expressed visually or mathematically (e.g., in an equation) into words.	
Assess the extent to which the reasoning and evidence in a text support the author's claim or a recommendation for solving a scientific or technical problem.	
Compare and contrast findings presented in a text to those from other sources (including their own experiments), noting when the findings support or contradict previous explanations or accounts.	
By the end of grade 10, read and comprehend science/technical texts in the grades 9–10 text complexity band independently and proficiently.	

APPENDIX

What You're Already Doing in Science and Technical Subjects for Grades 11–12

TABLE A6 Science and Technical Subjects Grades, 11–12

Grades 11–12	What You're Already Doing
Cite specific textual evidence to support analysis of science and technical texts, attending to important distinctions the author makes and to any gaps or inconsistencies in the account.	
Determine the central ideas or conclusions of a text; summarize complex concepts, processes, or information presented in a text by paraphrasing them in simpler but still accurate terms.	
Follow precisely a complex multistep procedure when carrying out experiments, taking measurements, or performing technical tasks; analyze the specific results based on explanations in the text.	
Determine the meaning of symbols, key terms, and other domain-specific words and phrases as they are used in a specific scientific or technical context relevant to *grades 11–12 texts and topics*.	

Appendix A6

Analyze how the text structures information or ideas into categories or hierarchies, demonstrating understanding of the information or ideas.	
Analyze the author's purpose in providing an explanation, describing a procedure, or discussing an experiment in a text, identifying important issues that remain unresolved.	
Integrate and evaluate multiple sources of information presented in diverse formats and media (e.g., quantitative data, video, multimedia) in order to address a question or solve a problem.	
Evaluate the hypotheses, data, analysis, and conclusions in a science or technical text, verifying the data when possible and corroborating or challenging conclusions with other sources of information	
Synthesize information from a range of sources (e.g., texts, experiments, simulations) into a coherent understanding of a process, phenomenon, or concept, resolving conflicting information when possible	
By the end of grade 12, read and comprehend science/technical texts in the grades 11–CCR text complexity band independently and proficiently.	

APPENDIX

Verb Switching

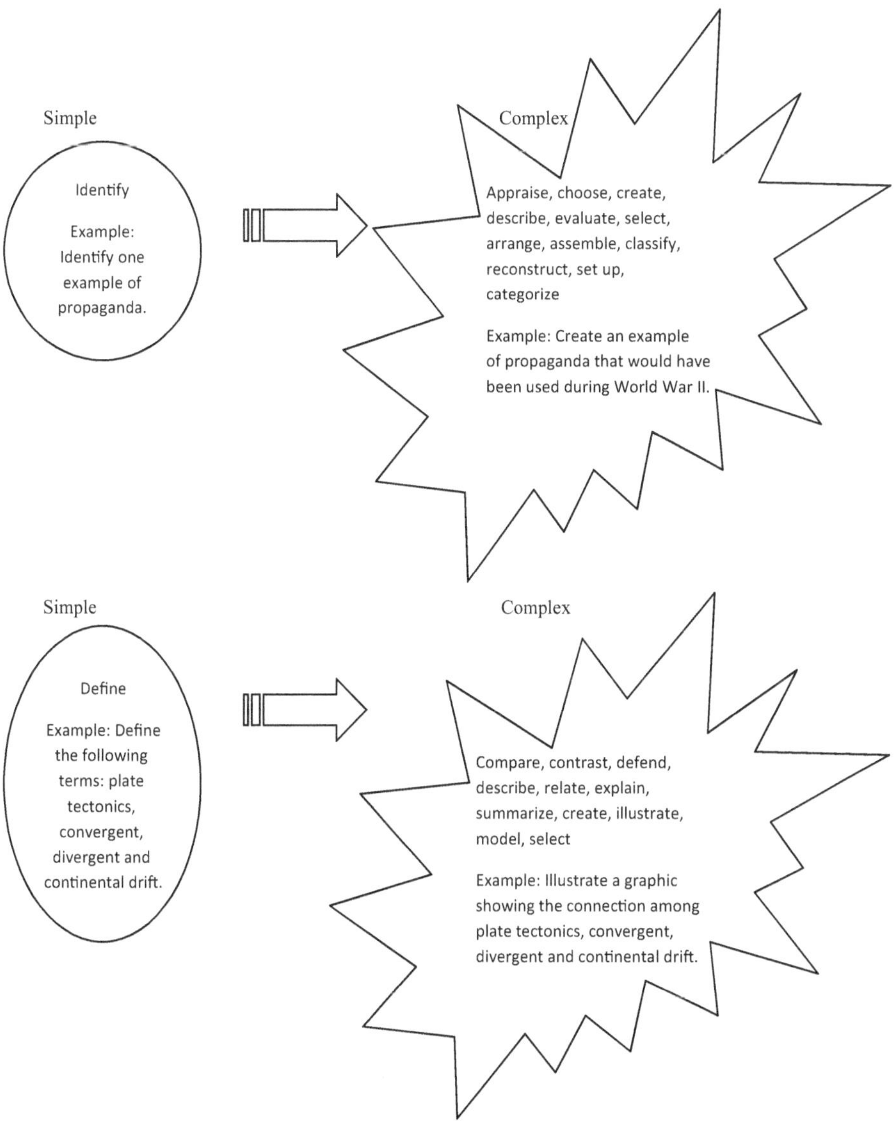

Simple

Identify

Example: Identify one example of propaganda.

Complex

Appraise, choose, create, describe, evaluate, select, arrange, assemble, classify, reconstruct, set up, categorize

Example: Create an example of propaganda that would have been used during World War II.

Simple

Define

Example: Define the following terms: plate tectonics, convergent, divergent and continental drift.

Complex

Compare, contrast, defend, describe, relate, explain, summarize, create, illustrate, model, select

Example: Illustrate a graphic showing the connection among plate tectonics, convergent, divergent and continental drift.

FIGURE A7 Verb Switching

Appendix A7

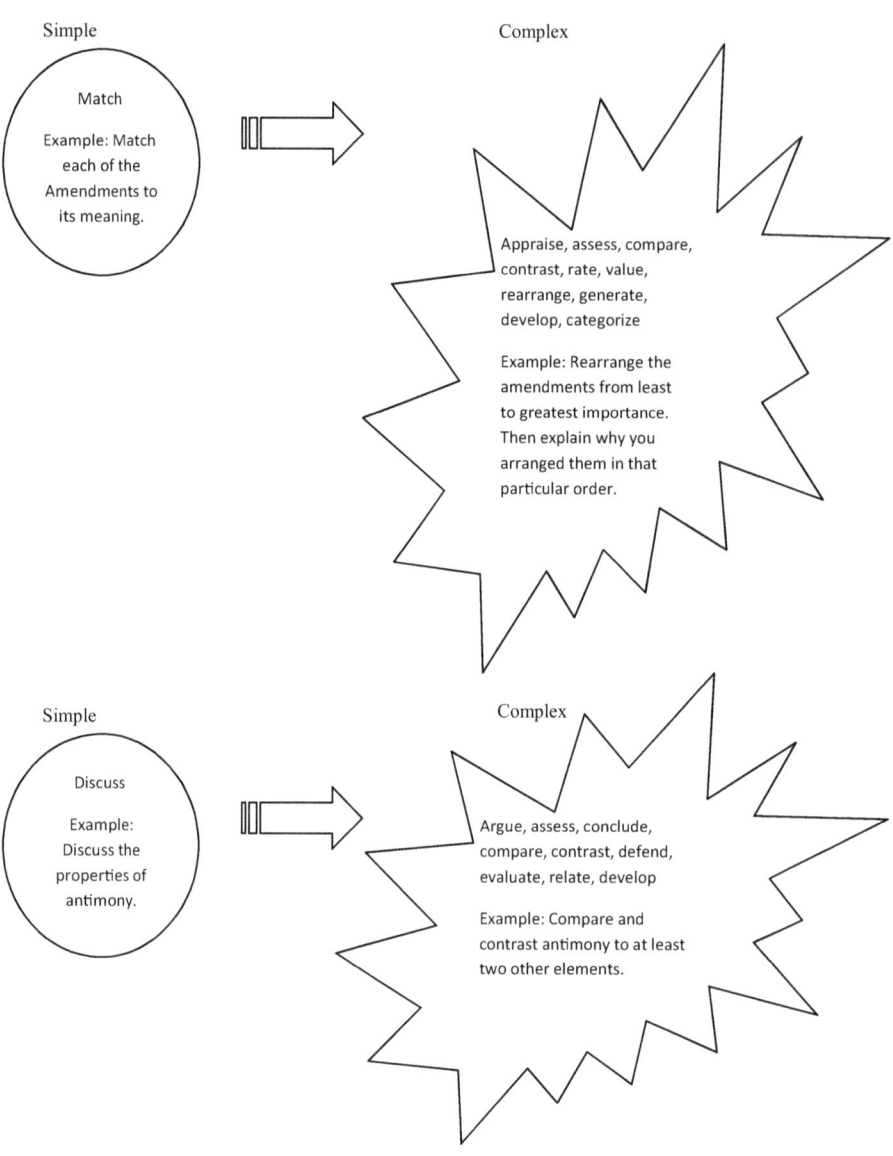

FIGURE A7 (Continued)

APPENDIX

Unit Planning Sheet

TABLE A8 Unit Plan

Focus Standards (no more than 3 or 4)	Content Focus	
Writing Activities	Reading Activities	
	Primary	Secondary

Appendix A8

Speaking and Listening/Collaboration Opportunites	Projects
Multimedia/Visual Information	Assessments
	Formative Summative
Possible Enrichment	Critical Thinking Questions

APPENDIX

Declaration of Independence Worksheet

Declaration of Independence

Objectives: Students will demonstrate the ability to . . .

    Compare and contrast text features, including format and headers in terms of their structure and purpose.
    Identify organizational structure and evaluate its effectiveness.
    Compare and contrast the treatment, scope and organization of ideas from different sources on the same topic.
    Assess the adequacy and appropriateness of an author's details.
    Identify the author's purpose and intended audience for the text.
    Analyze the author's argument, perspective or viewpoint and explain the development of key points.
    Recognize how writers cite facts and present opinions in informational text.

Use the Declaration of Independence to answer the following questions:

1. List the four headings from the Declaration of Independence. Then state the purpose of each heading. Explain why you think this heading is appropriate.

TABLE A9.1A Declaration of Independence

Heading	Purpose	Is Heading Appropriate?	Support Your Answer.

Appendix A9

2. Assess the organizational structure of the Declaration of Independence.
3. Describe how the Patriots and Loyalists are portrayed in *Chains*. Compare that to how each is portrayed in the Declaration of Independence. (Think, good guys, bad guys.)

TABLE A9.1B *Chains* and the Declaration of Independence

	Chains	Declaration of Independence
Patriots		
Loyalists		

4. Who is the intended audience of the Declaration of Independence, the whole world, the king, the British, the Americans? Cite two examples directly from the text that justify your answer.
5. Identify and describe the purpose of the Declaration of Independence. In your opinion, was the purpose met? Cite at least three details from at least two different sources to support your answer.
6. How do the details within the List of Grievances adequately support the resolution posed by the Patriots? Defend your answer with details from the text.
7. Cite four words, phrases or sentences that show the author's opinions.

    Ex.: "the merciless, Indian savages"—the author obviously does not think highly of Native Americans. I can infer this because of the words "merciless" and "savage."

    1.
    2.
    3.
    4.

APPENDIX

Graphic Organizer for Citing the Text

Topic_____

Source

I selected this source because
_____
_____

Central Ideas/Summary of Text
_____
_____
_____
_____

Direct Quote and Page #	Direct Quote and Page #	Direct Quote and Page #

FIGURE A10 Citing the Text

APPENDIX

Blank All A's Chart for History/Social Studies, Grades 6–8

TABLE A11 History/Social Studies, Grades 6–8

Grades 6–8	Absorb	Analyze	Argue	Apply
1. Cite specific textual evidence to support analysis of primary and secondary sources.				
2. Determine the central ideas or conclusions of a text; provide an accurate summary of the text distinct from prior knowledge or opinions.				
3. Identify key steps in a text's description of a process related to history/social studies.				
4. Determine the meaning of words and phrases as they are used in a text, including vocabulary specific to domains related to history/social studies.				

5. Describe how a text presents information (e.g., sequentially, comparatively, causally).				
6. Identify aspects of a text that reveal an author's point of view or purpose (e.g., loaded language, inclusion or avoidance of particular facts).				
7. Integrate visual information (e.g., in charts, graphs, photographs, videos, or maps) with other information in print and digital texts.				
8. Distinguish among fact, opinion, and reasoned judgment in a text.				
9. Analyze the relationship between a primary and secondary source on the same topic.				

APPENDIX

Blank All A's Chart for History/Social Studies, Grades 9–10

TABLE A12 History/Social Studies, Grades 9–10

Grades 9–10	Absorb	Analyze	Argue	Apply
1. Cite specific textual evidence to support analysis of primary and secondary sources, attending to such features as the date and origin of the information.				
2. Determine the central ideas or information of a primary or secondary source; provide an accurate summary of how key events or ideas develop over the course of the text.				
3. Analyze in detail a series of events described in a text; determine whether earlier events caused later ones or simply preceded them.				
4. Determine the meaning of words and phrases as they are used in a text, including vocabulary describing political, social, or economic aspects of history/social science.				

5. Analyze how a text uses structure to emphasize key points or advance an explanation or analysis.				
6. Compare the point of view of two or more authors for how they treat the same or similar topics, including which details they include and emphasize in their respective accounts.				
7. Integrate quantitative or technical analysis (e.g., charts, research data) with qualitative analysis in print or digital text.				
8. Assess the extent to which the reasoning and evidence in a text support the author's claims.				
9. Compare and contrast treatments of the same topic in several primary and secondary sources.				
10. By the end of grade 10, read and comprehend history/social studies texts in the grades 9–10 text complexity band independently and proficiently.				

APPENDIX

Blank All A's Chart for History/Social Studies, Grades 11–12

TABLE A13 History and Social Studies, Grades 11–12

Grades 11–12	Absorb	Analyze	Argue	Apply
1. Cite specific textual evidence to support analysis of primary and secondary sources, connecting insights gained from specific details to an understanding of the text as a whole.				
2. Determine the central ideas or information of a primary or secondary source; provide an accurate summary that makes clear the relationships among the key details and ideas.				
3. Evaluate various explanations for actions or events and determine which explanation best accords with textual evidence, acknowledging where the text leaves matters uncertain.				
4. Determine the meaning of words and phrases as they are used in a text, including analyzing how an author uses and refines the meaning of a key term over the course of a text (e.g., how Madison defines *faction* in *Federalist* No. 10).				

5. Analyze in detail how a complex primary source is structured, including how key sentences, paragraphs, and larger portions of the text contribute to the whole.				
6. Evaluate authors' differing points of view on the same historical event or issue by assessing the authors' claims, reasoning, and evidence.				
7. Integrate and evaluate multiple sources of information presented in diverse formats and media (e.g., visually, quantitatively, as well as in words) in order to address a question or solve a problem.				
8. Evaluate an author's premises, claims, and evidence by corroborating or challenging them with other information.				
9. Integrate information from diverse sources, both primary and secondary, into a coherent understanding of an idea or event, noting discrepancies among sources.				
10. By the end of grade 12, read and comprehend history/social studies texts in the grades 11–CCR text complexity band independently and proficiently.				

APPENDIX

A14

Blank All A's Chart for Science and Technical Subjects, Grades 6–8

TABLE A14 Science and Technical Subjects, Grades 6–8

Grades 6–8	Absorb	Analyze	Argue	Apply
1. Cite specific textual evidence to support analysis of science and technical texts.				
2. Determine the central ideas or conclusions of a text; provide an accurate summary of the text distinct from prior knowledge or opinions.				
3. Follow precisely a multistep procedure when carrying out experiments, taking measurements, or performing technical tasks.				
4. Determine the meaning of symbols, key terms, and other domain-specific words and phrases as they are used in a specific scientific or technical context relevant to *grades 6–8 texts and topics*.				

5. Analyze the structure an author uses to organize a text, including how the major sections contribute to the whole and to an understanding of the topic.				
6. Analyze the author's purpose in providing an explanation, describing a procedure, or discussing an experiment in a text.				
7. Integrate quantitative or technical information expressed in words in a text with a version of that information expressed visually (e.g., in a flowchart, diagram, model, graph, or table).				
8. Distinguish among facts, reasoned judgment based on research findings, and speculation in a text.				
9. Compare and contrast the information gained from experiments, simulations, video, or multimedia sources with that gained from reading a text on the same topic.				
10. By the end of grade 8, read and comprehend science/technical texts in the grades 6–8 text complexity band independently and proficiently.				

APPENDIX

Blank All A's Chart for Science and Technical Subjects, Grades 9–10

TABLE A15 Science and Technical Subjects, Grades 9–10

Grades 9–10	Absorb	Analyze	Argue	Apply
1. Cite specific textual evidence to support analysis of science and technical texts, attending to the precise details of explanations or descriptions.				
2. Determine the central ideas or conclusions of a text; trace the text's explanation or depiction of a complex process, phenomenon, or concept; provide an accurate summary of the text.				
3. Follow precisely a complex multistep procedure when carrying out experiments, taking measurements, or performing technical tasks, attending to special cases or exceptions defined in the text.				
4. Determine the meaning of symbols, key terms, and other domain-specific words and phrases as they are used in a specific scientific or technical context relevant to *grades 9–10 texts and topics*.				

5. Analyze the structure of the relationships among concepts in a text, including relationships among key terms (e.g., *force, friction, reaction force, energy*).				
6. Analyze the author's purpose in providing an explanation, describing a procedure, or discussing an experiment in a text, defining the question the author seeks to address.				
7. Translate quantitative or technical information expressed in words in a text into visual form (e.g., a table or chart) and translate information expressed visually or mathematically (e.g., in an equation) into words.				
8. Assess the extent to which the reasoning and evidence in a text support the author's claim or a recommendation for solving a scientific or technical problem.				
9. Compare and contrast findings presented in a text to those from other sources (including their own experiments), noting when the findings support or contradict previous explanations or accounts.				
10. By the end of grade 10, read and comprehend science/technical texts in the grades 9–10 text complexity band independently and proficiently.				

APPENDIX

Blank All A's Chart for Science and Technical Subjects, Grades 11–12

TABLE A16 Science and Technical Subjects, Grades 11–12

Grades 11–12	Absorb	Analyze	Argue	Apply
1. Cite specific textual evidence to support analysis of science and technical texts, attending to important distinctions the author makes and to any gaps or inconsistencies in the account.				
2. Determine the central ideas or conclusions of a text; summarize complex concepts, processes, or information presented in a text by paraphrasing them in simpler but still accurate terms.				
3. Follow precisely a complex multistep procedure when carrying out experiments, taking measurements, or performing technical tasks; analyze the specific results based on explanations in the text.				
4. Determine the meaning of symbols, key terms, and other domain-specific words and phrases as they are used in a specific scientific or technical context relevant to *grades 11–12 texts and topics*.				

5. Analyze how the text structures information or ideas into categories or hierarchies, demonstrating understanding of the information or ideas.				
6. Analyze the author's purpose in providing an explanation, describing a procedure, or discussing an experiment in a text, identifying important issues that remain unresolved.				
7. Integrate and evaluate multiple sources of information presented in diverse formats and media (e.g., quantitative data, video, multimedia) in order to address a question or solve a problem.				
8. Evaluate the hypotheses, data, analysis, and conclusions in a science or technical text, verifying the data when possible and corroborating or challenging conclusions with other sources of information.				
9. Synthesize information from a range of sources (e.g., texts, experiments, simulations) into a coherent understanding of a process, phenomenon, or concept, resolving conflicting information when possible.				
10. By the end of grade 12, read and comprehend science/technical texts in the grades 11–CCR text complexity band independently and proficiently.				

APPENDIX

Graphic Connections Organizer

TABLE A17 Connections Organizer

Topic: _____

Directions: In each column, make a connection from the text/content to the topic or item listed in the heading. Then explain the relationship or connection, and cite evidence in the text that led you to make the connection.

	Connection	Relationship	Text that led me to making this connection
TV Show			
Movie			
Place			
Song			
Different Content Area			
Video Game, Personal Experience or Free Choice			

APPENDIX

Outline for Argumentative Writing or Debate

Topic: _____

Argument or Claim:

Intended Audience:

Purpose:

Reason 1: _____

Fact or Support: _____

Citation: _____

Counterargument

How I will address counterargument

FIGURE A18: Outline for Argumentative Writing or Debate

Reason 2: _____
_____

    Fact or Support: _____
    _____

    Citation: _____
    _____

Counterargument	→	How I will address counterargument

Reason 3: _____
_____

    Fact or Support: _____
    _____

    Citation: _____
    _____

Counterargument	→	How I will address counterargument

Conclusion/Possible Solutions: _____

FIGURE A18: (Continued)

TABLE A18 Outline for Argumentative Writing or Debate

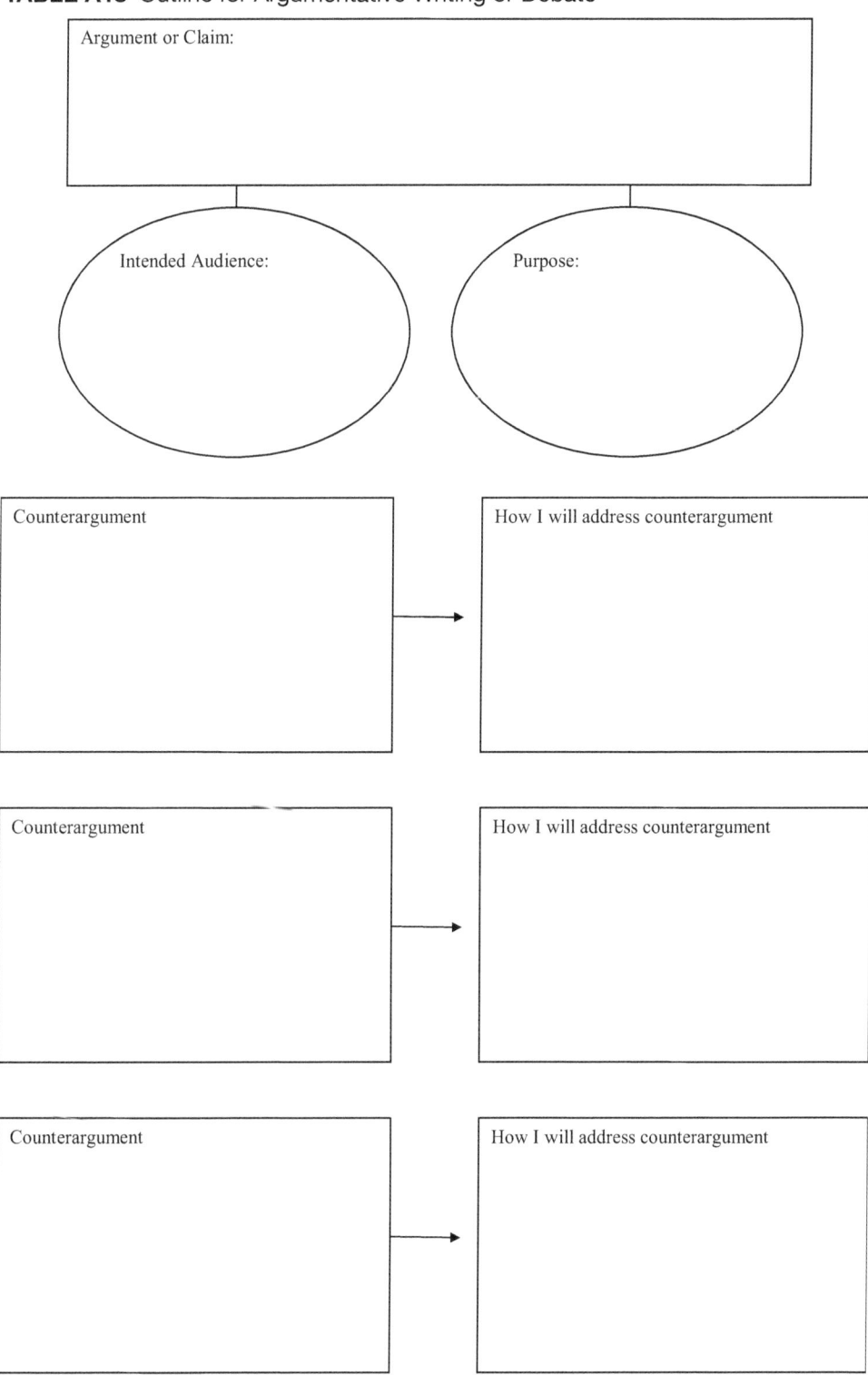

Appendix A18

Daily Lesson Plan Sheets

Teacher: Subject: Unit: Date:

	Goal(s):	Activities		Materials:
Monday		Students will	Teacher will	
	Objectives:			Evaluation Procedure(s):
Tuesday	Goal(s):	Activities		Materials:
		Students will	Teacher will	
	Objectives:			Evaluation Procedure(s):
Wednesday	Goal(s):	Activities		Materials:
		Students will	Teacher will	
	Objectives:			Evaluation Procedure(s):

Appendix A18

	Goal(s):	Activities		Materials:
Thursday		Students will	Teacher will	
	Objectives:			Evaluation Procedure(s):
Friday	Goal(s):	Activities		Materials:
		Students will	Teacher will	
	Objectives:			Evaluation Procedure(s):

161

For Product Safety Concerns and Information please contact our EU representative GPSR@taylorandfrancis.com
Taylor & Francis Verlag GmbH, Kaufingerstraße 24, 80331 München, Germany

www.ingramcontent.com/pod-product-compliance
Lightning Source LLC
Chambersburg PA
CBHW081421230426
43668CB00016B/2306